Everybody needs a paw paw. Aaron is bles[...] is in sharing learned lessons. His stories are timeless, insightful, [...] for his family and friends and anyone else that has observed his love for both.

Storytelling and letter writing are transparent ways to show every side of life- the funny, sad, proud, and rewarding. For generations past family legacies and lessons learned were shared through telling stories on the porch, on the couch, or playing in the yard. Few families these days take time to reminisce, reflect, and rewind. Dr. Porch does that with the written words that come alive in his letters

Written letters can never be forgotten or unread. They are wonderful insights from decades of life, hundreds of experiences that have meaningful lessons, and give future generations a priceless gift of memories. The offering of transparency is rare and vulnerable but these are ingredients for the longevity of life and memorable stories.

D. Tony Rankin
Counseling and Family Specialist
PO Box 728
Brentwood, TN 37024
(615)371-8136; (800)558-2090
trankin@tnbaptist.org

In today's fast-moving society, *The Paw Paw Letters: Life Lessons for Aaron* provides the reader with a refreshing change of pace. Aaron will certainly become aware of his secure heritage in these stories from his grandfather. Dr. Porch's stories depict honesty, commitment, and work ethic as necessary components for building a strong foundation of faith, stability, and hope.

--- Debbie Higdon, Aaron's Fourth Grade Teacher, Currey Ingram Academy

"Dr. Porch has been blessed with an amazing gift for telling stories with a spiritual purpose. Through each story, he allows the reader to look into a rich part of history and connect the important values that are being quickly forgotten in our world today. Dr. Porch shares with us the love, humor, and life lessons that should be passed on to the next generation. This is a wonderful book for teachers, ministry leaders and parents – not only for the important life lessons that will be found in each story - but also to encourage and inspire us to share our own stories with our children. "

Valerie J. Davidson
Preschool/Special Education Specialist
P.O. Box 728
Brentwood, TN 37024-0728
1.800.558.2090
615.371.2082   CELL 615.347.4671   FAX   615.301.0613
vdavidson@tnbaptist.org   www.tnchildhood.org

THE PAW PAW LETTERS

Life Lessons for Aaron from A Good Place
with Wise Folks During Hard Times.

JAMES PORCH

CROSSBOOKS
PUBLISHING

CrossBooks™
A Division of LifeWay
1663 Liberty Drive
Bloomington, IN 47403
www.crossbooks.com
Phone: 1-866-879-0502

First published by CrossBooks 1/25/2011

ISBN: 978-1-6150-7678-9 (sc)
ISBN: 978-1-6150-7691-8 (dj)

Library of Congress Control Number: 2010942001

Printed in the United States of America

This book is printed on acid-free paper.

In loving memory
of the grace of Big Milton and Miss Lillian.
Throughout the 1940s and 1950s,
you raised me right.

Blessings

No writer should claim sole authorship. Each emerging
message includes the labors of other contributing folk.

Thank you, Mimi, (Kelly, my wife) for encouraging this risk and
for your editorial perspective graced with grammatical candor.

Thank you, Lonnie Wilkey, a Barnabas friend
who championed the original idea.

Thank you, Phyllis Bates, friend and executive assistant, for nurturing
my focus lest other stuff displaced my passion for the Paw Paw message.

Thank you, church folk across Tennessee, for asking, "When
are you going to write another Paw Paw Letter?"

Contents

Introduction to The Paw Paw Letters

Personal values nurture character, or character determines personal values? Oh well, as in the adage of the chicken or the egg, the debate may never end. My prevailing concern rests more in the development of values in children struggling in the 21st century to maintain innocence while bombarded by a secular environment. Christian parenting today goes up against the power of time-absence from kids due to job demands, divorce, the lure of pleasure, and, tragically, neglect. Intentional value teaching, especially by example, suffers due to fatigue and even more the absence of prevalent solid, non-negotiable values abiding in the character of many parents.

My previous paragraph may appear harsh. No indictment is meant. Rather, give the issue a chance for personal reflection as I seek to offer a value teaching help. At the outset, I must claim sole responsibility for this writing. This is my story of my value system, still in development, which began during childhood and adolescence in a good place with wise folks during hard times.

I was a child and teenager of the first generation whose values benefited from the Great Depression of the 1930s. Born in 1941, the year the Great Depression officially ended (ha), my daily life (until I left for college in 1959) developed in the blessing and nurture of parents and community who had "made it through." That phrase expressed the primary hope of Mississippi folk from 1929 and on.

My folks, known in the community as Milton and Lillian, differed greatly in age. They married in 1935 in the middle of the Great Depression. Dad was 47. Mama was 25. She, a high-school graduate and one of 11 children, grew up on family-owned land. He, illiterate by lack of education opportunities, lived as part of a tenant family on other people's land and began hard work in the cotton fields as a child. Dad's blacksmith skills generated out of his head and through his calloused hands. Mom, a nurse, carried a life-long passion to help hurting folks as expressed in her soft hands. "Big Milton," his nick-name following my birth, personified authenticity, extreme individualism and integrity while Mom, quite a bit political, thrived through diligence and determination in pushing out her envelope.

The times I speak of encompassed an era not bad—just hard. After all, local folks did not cause the Depression. Quite the contrary, a bunch of greedy rich folks up north on Wall Street collapsed the economy and left us to make it through hard times. For us, dwelling on the reason seemed ridiculous and a mere waste of time and energy. The era moved along from economic interruption to a season mixed with determination, toleration, and sometimes despair to a point of embracing the growing theme, "Mr. Roosevelt's going to save us all." Yet not all bought into the savior idea. Pelahatchie, a dot on the map, did not catch the eyes of Washington, except for the day Eleanor Roosevelt's touring train made a whistle stop passing through our town on the Illinois Central Railroad. My Daddy boycotted her visit, but that's another story.

The place challenged description and defied definition. Pelahatchie, Choctaw for Crooked Creek, while legally incorporated by name, denoted a community. Outsiders made the pilgrimage into town primarily to visit relatives or friends or to shop on Saturday. In essence, to the less than 1,000 residents, the culture offered few gates into a nearly closed society. I believe our heritage of difficult living extending back to Reconstruction birthed this mentality, and the Great Depression crystallized the effort. Attention to needs, reliance on neighbors, adjusted living almost on a daily basis, and hope that hard times would end seemed, as I remember, to displace gossip, nosiness, and even church fusses. After all, you were either Baptist, Methodist, or nothing (except for Dr. Johnson, our Catholic doctor, who more than once saved my life).

Today, the remains of most of my hometown heroes rest in the local cemetery across from the schoolhouse. Often at night, their faces race through my mind, a race I interrupt to relive an old moment and to thank God for hugging people, connecting people, teaching folks, witnessing folks, affirming folks, and…just good folks.

Hopefully, as you read the previous paragraphs, you begin to seek the purpose of this reminiscence.

Today, little if any impact of the 1930's *Great Depression* effect influences American culture. I am a debtor to that era and believe intensely the time, place, and folk all interwoven can assist God's people in introducing and nurturing Christian values to our children. There was something special about the time that is good for today.

I hold a more precious reason—my grandson, Aaron, may have only one shot at exposure to value development as influenced by the Great Depression era. I am, I have, I carry a haunting passion to pass on to him valuable lessons from an age long ago that by the grace of God nurtured my life development. And so, I have written

The Paw Paw Letters,
Life Lessons
for
Aaron
from
a Good Place with Wise Folks During Hard Times

I will write, with a prayer, to draw pictures in his mind of valued days of my life with the hope to bless his season.

A Place Called Pelahatchie

Rehoboth Hill
Cane Ridge, TN

Dear Aaron,

Pelahatchie, Mississippi, my boyhood hometown, really exists! Paw Paw's very unique hometown could never be merely a product of anyone's imagination. The very different place in the 1940s and 50s, quite vivid in my memory, assuredly even now feeds my passion to pursue my own God given uniqueness in responding to His will for my life.

I hope in these letters to convey both bits of humor and consciousness of celebration, while peering into a few of the windows of my childhood town life.

Sometime in 1830, Choctaw Indians and representatives of the United States Government met at a place called Doak's Stand, and the Indians signed a treaty ceding 5 ½ million acres of land to the state of Mississippi. Nearby, a very crooked creek washed through the loam soil. The Indians called the tributary Pelahatchie, and the name displaced Doak's Stand. A few years before the Civil War scourge of General Sherman, a pioneer, Mr. G.F. Span, laid out a town around a 300-acre plot. Later, the Mississippi legislature acted to incorporate the entity named Pelahatchie.

I discovered Crooked Creek sometime late in June, 1941, a few days after my birth. The trip home from the hospital covered 8 ½ miles from Morton, the next town over to the east and the site of the nearest hospital. Mom and Dad carried me home to a white frame house on Munsterman Street (gravel road). This was pre-air conditioning time so, as the practice was, a sheer cloth was thrown over the baby bed to deflect the flies and mosquitoes. During the next 18 years, my world would revolve around that little town, and upon graduation from high school my travels had never exceeded 50 miles from home.

For me, there is absolutely no need to waste space or words on the inadequacy of the place, cry over deficiencies, or seek pity from a neglected childhood. Rather emphatically, my life is a song of ascents for the blessing of a small hometown and the opportunity to celebrate big memories to my grandson.

The point where federal Highway 80 and the town's Brook Street intersected at the only red and green traffic light became the center of the community. Later the electric signal, by action of the mayor and Board of Aldermen, would be upgraded to a red, yellow, and green light. Caution hit our town much later than stop and go. Major growth began in the town following the increase of horse and mule drawn wagons and buggies, and pedestrian and motor traffic from the surrounding communities of Holly Bush, Barefoot Springs, Rehoboth, Shiloh, Lodebar, Clarksburg, Gulde, Andrew Chapel, Pisgah, Crossroads, Ludlow, and Branch. Most pilgrims made their trip on Saturday, thereby making the Sabbath a make-it or break-it day for merchants.

The area included a variety of grocery stores, each unique because of its commodities. Usually folk chose the specific grocery store on the basis of the reputation of the grocer for giving true weight. Many items in those days were sold fresh and thereby required weighing. Some grocery store merchants were known to hang a thumb over the scales and inflate the weight, thereby raising the prices. I often heard grocers referred to as men of the big or small thumb.

Specifically, I visualize Mr. G's Fairway Store. Around town, the proprietor was renowned for keeping a fresh stalk of bananas and a knife nearby. Somehow, he had a contact with a supplier that ensured a year round supply of "nanners."

Just down the street from Mr. G's, Mr. B's General Mercantile drew quite a clientele. We shopped there quite a bit. In the rear of the store reigned a gigantic motor bolted securely to a counter. Different attachments to the motor enabled the grocer to grind coffee, make hamburger meat, or stuff sausage. It simply was a matter of changing the attachments. The store contained no sink or washing apparatus. The specific use grinders were merely kept in the meat cooler thereby retarding, I suppose, any bacteria or germs.

A third store, Mr. W's, a back street establishment accessible by two screen doors and shunned by many of the Pelahatchie "upper crust," included an adjacent grist mill. A large clientele would gather on Saturday afternoon attracted to the all afternoon live country music. Our family, "lower crust," depended on the grist mill as our only source of fresh corn meal.

To the best of my knowledge, restaurant sanitary inspection never reached town during my tenure. This is not in any way to reflect on Miss Eunice's Café. While our family seldom ate out, I savored and drooled over her 10-cent hamburgers. She began with hand pressed patties. The fresh bun was placed over the cooking patty to soak up the grease. Once the patty was done, mustard, pickle, and a whole slice of onion were added. No hamburger ever tasted any better than those prepared by Miss Eunice.

The town did include another "restaurant." The café was merely referred unaffectionately, to as Rube's. His wife, the cook, took care of all the activity in the kitchen. Mr. Rube sat by the cash register, swatting flies and smoking one cigarette after the other, thereby contaminating the restaurant.

Pelahatchie featured limited service facilities. Major car repairs demanded the help of mechanics either at the De Soto or Chevrolet dealership. Most people changed their own oil, fixed flats, tuned engines by the sound of the motor, or performed minor repairs during those hard times.

Holmes' Barber Shop, featuring two chairs, specialized in quick 50-cent Saturday afternoon haircuts including a liberal application of Rose Red Hair Tonic, provided you endured the wait. The Saturday trip home for many folk included picking up a block of ice freshly frozen and trucked from far away Jackson 25 miles to the west. My Uncle Tot's ice house also catered to the hard working pulpwood laborers from across the railroad track. He sold Pine Burr bologna, cinnamon rolls, hoop cheese, and a variety of sardines, tripe, pig's feet, and other luncheon meat. He cut his bologna with a cold knife stored in the refrigerator, once again to retard bacteria and germs.

A major service addition came to town when C.C. built his locker plant. For a monthly fee, you could rent secured space in the freezer to store vegetables, fruits, and meats. To Mama's delight one day, Dad rented a locker so our family could progress beyond total canning to the luxury of freezing food. While commenting on cold, I must announce that air conditioning invaded our town first in the Rankin County Bank.

Subsequently, a fear spread across many folk believing that the cold air, especially in the hot summertime, would produce pneumonia.

Dad's blacksmith shop, located downtown, gave me the opportunity to frequently visit two very special places. Mrs. Dora Lee and her husband operated a combination service station, barber shop, and grocery store. Occasionally Dad would pitch me a nickel for either a candy bar or cold drink. I'm still intrigued by Mrs. Dora Lee's patience as I stood in front of the racks of Baby Ruth, Butterfinger, Snickers, Milky Way, Hershey Bars (milk chocolate or with almonds), ZagNut, Zero Bar, Butternut, and Stage Planks, pondering my decision on the important purchase.

Dad had wisely chosen the spot for his blacksmith shop next door to the Rankin County Hardware. This enabled him to conveniently buy materials. The store, owned by Mr. Ellis, became one of my favorite play places. Most of the time, the elderly gentleman, a Baptist, sat in his office chair behind a big pot bellied coal stove, summer or winter, and slept with his pipe in his mouth. His daughter, Miss Beulah, handled all of the book work, and a gentleman simply known as "Mr. Fountain" handled the business in the store. As far as Mr. Ellis was concerned, as his buddy I had free run of his entire store. One afternoon he received a supply of BB guns. The articles arrived late in November as he planned to feature them for Christmas. Instantly, I began my campaign to seek a Santa Claus BB gun. That will be included in a later letter, Aaron.

In our town, no place offered more intrigue to an eight year-old than the loafer's bench. Through the week, the wood frame antique sat outside the post office. Many occupants either walked with one or two canes or crutches. At apparently what he thought was the appropriate time, Dad explained to me these gentlemen suffered a condition called Jake Leg. Mississippi for a long time was a dry state—no legal beverage alcohol sales. Nevertheless, alcohol illegally, literally, and freely flowed throughout the communities. Sometime during the era of The Great Depression, a poisoned batch of Jamaica Gin arrived at the Tip Toe Inn, a joint near town. The gentlemen who imbibed experienced a creeping paralysis affecting them for the rest of their lives. This was my first encounter with the consequences of wrong doing that can be everlasting.

Following the Friday sitting on the loafer's bench, the furniture article would be moved up to the corner of Highway 80 and Brook Street.

Throughout the weekend, young boys would sit and gather around the loafer's bench to talk to people stopping at the red light. For many, these contacts provided initial opportunities for outreach to the big world beyond Crooked Creek.

While many other businesses occupied locations in our town, no place conveyed the uniqueness of Butter Bell's Store. Over the years, the old wood framed store gradually leaned to the right, requiring the placing of telephone poles to prevent the building from falling across an alley and onto another nearby store. Mr. Bell sold everything, pots and pans, overalls, brogans, flannel underwear, hats, bonnets, and patent medicines on the front porch of his emporium. According to a long established rumor, he allowed no one inside the store. Many mysteries surrounded the place. One I remember was the insistent rumor that Mr. Bell slept in a coffin.

He maintained the town contract to sell the state newspaper, *The Clarion Ledger*. Each morning and afternoon seven days a week, whistling his personal song, the old gentleman would meet the bus at Purvis' Service Station to sell papers to riders. Mr. Bell sold most of his papers just as the bus pulled away from the station, thereby providing buyers with papers days or weeks old, only to be discovered after leaving the station.

One day Mr. Bell did not open his business. The next day the door remained shut. Finally, the town fathers decided someone must invade the Bell store and try to find the proprietor. As the story developed, once inside they found racks and racks and stacks and stacks of newspapers completely filling the store. Near the end of a tunnel through the papers, the pioneers discovered a very sick Mr. Bell lying on a cot. He had no electricity, no running water, and thereby raised serious questions related to his lifestyle.

Aaron, as you read this letter, I'm sure you wonder if Paw Paw makes up any of this stuff. Absolutely not! All of this is absolutely, unconditionally the truth.

While the name Pelahatchie often raises a laugh at first hearing, those of us privileged to live in the town honor and revere the place. In essence, don't get on my bad side talkin' down my hometown.

You see, I knew a time and place of polite people. Men tipped their hats to women; "Mister," "Miss," and "Missus" permeated conversations. Only the pharmacy dispensed drugs. Public drunkenness meant quick jail time. Each family or home owner took care of his garbage and attended to his own litter. No store stayed open on Sunday. Only the passing through Illinois Central train broke the quietness of the night. Mr. P checked the oil and washed the windshield, even if daddy only bought two dollars worth of gas (six gallons). Kids could go to the store with a signed check, and parents trusted proprietors to fill in the correct amount. Most adults viewed an alone child as a ward for their protection. And, our flag never flew in the rain.

Passing on values with hope,

Paw Paw

A Trust Account Matters

Rehoboth Hill
Cane Ridge, TN

Dear Aaron,

Have you ever heard the church term Protracted Meeting? Of course not! You're growing up going to Sunday School, "Big Church," Mission Friends, Prayer Meeting, and Wednesday Night Supper. Protracted Meetings kind of went out of style after Paw Paw reached his teenage years. Nevertheless, I especially remember one in 1951—one I will *never* forget.

A Baptist Protracted Meeting began on a certain date and went on—and sometimes went on and on—until the preacher announced, "The meeting will end tomorrow night." The non-planned ending gave birth to the name "Protracted." I never could understand how the preacher knew to end the event in exactly 24 hours. Each year, Mom, Dad and I made the homecoming Sunday "all day preachin' and dinner-on-the-ground" at their respective home churches, Barefoot Springs and Rehoboth. The Barefoot meeting always began the second Sunday in August, and Rehoboth (eight miles away) preempted the sister or brother church by starting the third Sunday in July. These dates, scheduled on Heaven's calendar, could not be changed. Each originated to coincide with "layin' by" time for the farmers. Layin' by, when everything had been done that could be done to a crop, ushered in a season for folks to attend the morning and evening revival services out from under the pressure of unfinished farming. Years before, families would camp on the church grounds. The Shiloh Methodist District near my home town even now includes campground huts to lodge folks.

Okay, so you get the idea. Now I'll hone in on the Homecoming Protracted Meeting at the Rehoboth Baptist Church in Rankin County, Mississippi on the third Sunday in July of 1951. The morning service included spiffy

singing out of the *Broadman Hymnal* and loud preaching, producing a
ring around the collar on every white, starched and done-up shirt, despite
the fact of all the windows being raised to the top and every right and
left-hand Ott and Lee Funeral Home fan waving in high-wrist gear. By
dinner-on-the-grounds time (evidently an outreach feature), the crowd had
multiplied. Some of the ladies waited up to the last minute to arrive to
prevent serving up cold food. Chicken pie arrived in dishpans, 40-weight
tea cooled in a new zinc washtub with a 50-pound block of ice, and one
judged the banana pudding by the number of bubbles of sweet sweat on
the meringue. Fryin' chicken had been cut up in such a manner so that the
pulley bone—all white meat—got the first forks. Rehoboth church held
hard and fast to the Biblical mandate, "Let the little children come" first
in line. Barefoot Springs, eight miles away, majored more on the appetites
of the elders, and little children had to pick over chicken wings and necks
and scrape the bowls for bare sustenance.

My big trouble happened during the afternoon service, a special time
planned for the dedication of the church's new attic fan. That appliance
had remained idle during the morning service. Actually, it had never been
turned on except for a test by the installers. Oh, well, what Baptist would
breathe unconsecrated air? During lunch, yours truly and several of my
Porch cousins pled with our mamas for mercy from the afternoon service.
We actually convinced them to let us stay outside. My Daddy literally
wasn't too hot on my absence. After all, our family was listed for a $25
contribution to the fan fund. The covenant agreement with our parents was
that the forthcoming quality of our behavior during the afternoon must be
beyond reproach. This agreement included staying away from the church's
rainwater cistern directly across the road from the front door of the church.
The covered dirt water reservoir was in direct sight line from the pulpit. No
one went to the waterhole during the service unseen by the preacher.

After the Fan Committee stood for recognition, the name of each
contributor was read and my Uncle Charlie, chairman of the deacons,
read appropriate scripture from Acts 2; the pastor thanked God for the
increased comfort of God's people.

Don't get me wrong—this was serious business. If you have doubts, try
sitting in a Mississippi Baptist church in mid-July with no air flow of any
kind. The atmosphere promoted hell-fire preaching.

Now, accompanied by the steady hum of the fan and the sucking sound of moving air, the preacher tried to begin his sermon. Apparently, in frightful distress, he stopped and declared, "I cannot continue this sermon while those children are playing around that cistern across the road." Several men rushed to his aid, running the kids away from the shade of the pavilion over the cistern. Though obvious to everyone that the problem had been addressed, one returning deacon verbally assured the preacher that the problem would not reoccur and began to call the names of each guilty child. Even though my cousins and I remained behind the church playing, God forbid, in the cemetery, several of us were labeled. In my description, he simply affirmed, "One was that little Porch boy from Pelahatchie." My Daddy, quite embarrassed, shared all these details with me in our home living room following a silent ride that afternoon from what I thought was a great Homecoming Protracted Meeting Sunday.

After the descriptive indictment, my rotund father stood up and quickly pulled off his long, black belt. I still recall the popping sound as the leather slid through each belt loop. While knowing never to argue with him, I took a chance on honesty. Tearfully, with fright, I volunteered, "Daddy, I did not go to the cistern. I played in the cemetery." My ambivalent feelings awaited his response. He sat down, slumped over a bit, looked into my eyes and allowing moisture to creep down his cheek, he put his hand on my shoulder and firmly but quickly said, "James Milton, as far as I know you have never lied to me before. Son, I believe you." The end!

Well, not exactly. While the experience has remained a big memory, only years later did I understand my Daddy's response. In my words, evidently I had built up enough credits in my bank of trust with him that the dividend paid off.

Aaron, sometimes you can be blamed even when you're innocent. One of your best hopes will be to rely on past good character. You, with our Heavenly Father's help, can build such integrity.

Passing on values with hope,

Paw Paw

Becoming Real by His Grace

Rehoboth Hill
Cane Ridge, TN

Dear Aaron,

Guess what? All us — you, me, Mimi, and Mom Terri— all have something in common. Each of us had to endure a parent stopping and having a conversation with a friend or relative while as kids we waited through the eternity of the moment.

Our tactic to move on included "I've got to go to the bathroom. My feet hurt. I'm hot. I'm freezing. I'm feeling sick," all the while pulling on a hand or tugging at clothes. Absolutely nothing defied that crucial conversation. We felt ignored and forgotten while anger and pity ran up the scale. You want to say, "Momma or Daddy, don't you know what it's like down here? Doesn't the need of your precious darling take precedent over the weather, sick folks, politicians, and a mixture of 'have you heard about… or have you heard the one about…'?"

A parent seems to enter the "forgot you zone" with his world consisting of only the real estate big enough for four feet and a spittin' zone. Delaying a child in route is disgraceful, inconsiderate, and possibly borders on child abuse. Yes, my description announces my overreaction, except when you are a kid stopped in his tracks with no good purpose. I can never recall being consulted or even warned about the impromptu verbal encounter. How kind and sweet if I could have only heard, "James, here comes John Earl, David Leonard, Betty Jo, Maudine, Vesta, Miss Ola, Oscar David, Son Newell, Junior Thorntonberry, Betty Sue, Hattie Lyrah, or Big Bubba, and I need to stop and talk a little while." Oh, no! You just stop, wait, shift your weight, stretch, scratch, and in desperation, cry. The weeping thing rarely worked. On occasions, I even prayed for a small nosebleed. My best rescue came the day I pretended to swallow a bug and tried to throw up. I now believe the ability to hiccup on command could have been my best tool. While still holding memories of those immediate and necessary interruptions, I must confess to one that changed my life.

His name was _____ (these *Paw Paw Letters* are getting back home to Pelahatchie, so to "protect the innocent" I'll forgo his identity). Anyhow, Daddy and I walked out of the county courthouse one beautiful warm April afternoon. That Mississippi spring had developed far enough that I enjoyed the liberty of short pants and bare feet. Dad's bib overalls, rolled up denim shirt sleeves, and straw hat bearing numerous sweat rings served as background to the grease stains, cinder burns, and sweat marks indelibly etched on his clothes. They seemed to complement his large physique and enormous hands. Crossing the courthouse lawn, we approached a bulky fellow attired in a seersucker, tobacco-stained suit with multiple rings around the shirt collar, puffin' on a cigarette in desperate need of ash-flicking, and reeking with a sour smell. As my anxiety surged in an expectation of an interruption, he spoke, "Mornin' Milton, this here yo boy?" Proudly claiming parenthood, Dad moved toward our car, and "John Doe" kept talking. Dad's courtesy won out. For the next "season of eternity," (at least 15 minutes) the disheveled fellow verbally listed his notable family tree, narrated his heroism during the war (World War II), and offered his political connection help to my Dad. Suddenly, he leaned toward me and grabbed my shoulder. Frightened and afraid to move, I looked up to hear him tell me, "Boy, I'm a self-made man." Then he wobbly walked on into the courthouse. Dad, a bit irritated (maybe angry), rubbed his stubbled unshaved face (Dad shaved once a week whether he needed it or not) and remarked, "Yeah, and you made a mess." I remember my father's narrative of that conversation, both in humor and pity as he told John Doe's story many times.

I sincerely ascribe to the conviction that our Heavenly Father intends parents to be givers. This value I hold dearly as a recipient and provider. I received from my father an assortment of his blacksmith tools, artifacts left over from his experience as a soldier in World War I, a good name, and most of all his love and wisdom.

Only when I ran out of the pursuit of educational degrees did I struggle with the impact of the courthouse yard event. Repeatedly, I came back to ask who or what made me as I am and am becoming. Aaron, welcome such a struggle. Only in resolving or seeking to resolve the tension for your self can you approach the joy the Father intends for you in being just who you are.

You can't allow people, especially un-well meaning folk, to shape your life. You can undertake a lonely and desperate attempt to fashion your one life totally by your own plan, energy, and selfishness. Or, in surrender, you can welcome our Father's empowering grace to mold you in developing your life. An itinerant missionary in a moment of his blatant authenticity said, "I am what I am by the grace of God" (1 Corinthians 15:10). Aaron, our Heavenly Father led your Paw Paw to that verse a long, long time ago, and I'm still leaning on that truth to learn who I really am.

But the most meaningful of all is the memory and more that as a child and a teen I lived in the presence and care of a real person. His greatest fear of hypocrisy was losing the opportunity to just be himself.

Passing on values with hope,

Paw Paw

The MAKEDO Principle Learned Early

Rehoboth Hill
Cane Ridge, TN

Dear Aaron,

Well, time has come to announce one of our family secrets. From infancy, you have been carrying a germ. Aaron, your mother, has the Wal-Mart disease. Mimi and I cannot plead ignorance. She is afflicted by buying purses, and I carry the chronic malady of buying shirts. Actually, Paw Paw has another problem. At least twice a week, some job or "need" at Rehoboth (our home place) requires me to stop work and immediately drive quickly to Lowe's. (If Mimi and I ever move, we will live at least 100 miles from Lowe's or Home Depot.)

My summary, or analysis, of the family dilemma comes down to the fact that we live in the STUFF era. Literally we STUFFITES know STUFF is available in stores and over the internet. We want STUFF right now, and we pay to have STUFF right now! Don't be too hard on us. After all, resistance to marketing "designed for our better being" is difficult.

Now another announcement. Living every day only with necessary THINGS is tough. THINGS include what we have or don't have or have to do without that requires us to MAKEDO and still enjoy life. I hope you will read that sentence over and over, and in the King James fashion, "ponder" the meaning.

I am still struggling to help you appreciate MAKEDO in your amazing anything available world. Two of my childhood processes may help, sewing sack shirts and warming up leftovers.

The sack shirt production usually began, "Lillian, (my mother) I am going to the feed store." "Milton, (my daddy) wait, I will be ready in a few minutes."

Why would both of my parents have to make a routine short trip to buy chicken feed? Simple! Mama had to pick out the sacks. Back in the 1940's and 1950's, chicken feed was packed in 100-pound cotton sacks with colorful designs. I recall sacks bearing stripes, checks, flowers, and even kitties and doggies. Two of the same sacks made a shirt. Three matched sacks enabled a seamstress to sew a dress. Contrary to rumors, southern mothers did not make underwear from chicken feed sacks. Flour sack was the material of choice for undies.

When opening the sack, a delicate operation, great care was given to clipping the top sewed string. If properly cut, the entire sack (once the feed was emptied) could be unraveled in one seamless piece of cloth. Then came my feared assignment, "James, shake out those feed sacks." Quite a dusty and itchy job, especially in July and August.

Next, all sacks regardless of design went into a wash tub of cold water to soak. I don't remember why that step was necessary. They soaked until wash day (Monday).

Then Mama laundered the cloth in the old wringer tub washer with "Duz-Does It" detergent. Once the cloth was hung out on the backyard clothesline, the heavenly sun dried the sacks and by late afternoon the fresh clean- smelling material had been carefully folded and saved for sewing. Sometimes after the summer canning season, Mama would unfold her old treadle powered sewing machine and carefully lay out the newsprint pattern on the kitchen table. The ladies of the community passed the pattern around to each other to copy on newspaper with no regard for copyrights violations. After all, the depression era fostered the extreme of MAKEDO. The matching of stripes and other patterns, placing of pockets, and working button holes provided feed sack clothes that could be worn proudly as works of loving art. After Mama died, I searched the family home in quest of just one feed sack shirt. Sadly, those shirts exist now only in my memory and as a story of the value of MAKEDO.

As to leftovers, only Mimi's scratch banana pudding stands a chance in our house. Other leftovers grow dry or turn green in our refrigerator. In essence, we waste food.

Food on the table in Mississippi in the 40's and 50's became the same food on the table until and until . . . . . the matron of the house relegated edible items to the vessel whose contents were reserved for the nourishment of domestic swine. (Slop for the hogs.)

My mother, or "sweet mom" to her grandchildren, had mastered by way of her mother of 11 children the skill to bring new life to leftovers. A pod of pepper or fresh cut okra would wake up yesterday's butter beans or peas. New gravy could smother two-day old fried chicken and ensure vitality. Her cornbread, (no sugar allowed) needed only to be buttered and grilled in a skillet and a new crispy crust displaced the dry inner crumbs. And pie, if you pilled meringue high enough, the taste could not be lost. Oh well, the case for leftovers could go on and on, but I think you get the point.

Aaron, Mimi and I are in the process of recovering and renewing MAKEDO. We are in agreement that four essentials govern our everyday life at our Rehoboth home--duct tape, bungee cords, W-D40, and Pinesol, all available at Wal-Mart or Lowe's. Somehow equipped for those modern miracles, we can MAKEDO.

MAKEDO has a very strong affinity with Jesus' parable of the talents. Remember the one talent man. He chose not to MAKEDO with his lone talent and he surrendered the ability to MAKEDO. And even more as in the case of the other two men, the one talent man missed God's great surprise. Now that was a lost value. Talents increase according to our wise usage. I wonder if the first talent for all of God's people is to make do with what we have. If so, use your God-given skill and make do. Remember, God is big on surprises for faithfulness.

Passing on values with hope,

Paw Paw

The Pieces Can Come Together

Rehoboth Hill
Cane Ridge, TN

Dear Aaron,

The fading sign above my Dad's shop read "J.M. Porch, Blacksmith and Repair Shop." Having grown up in that setting, I hold many precious memory scenes of Dad at work repairing or fixing a farmer's broken, twisted, or malfunctioning equipment. I firmly believe my father possessed the gift of "fix it." I can still visualize friends of his shop bringing a broken plow, ax, hoe, shovel, or Jo blade handle to be replaced, or delivering a set of wagon wheels with cracked or broken spokes or loose tires, or even leading a pair of mules walking on one or more feet with thrown shoes, and especially the old wagon being towed down the alley leaning to the left or right due to a cracked axle. I recall vividly an African American farmer holding half of a doubletree in each hand, asking if the trace chain hooks and frizz iron could be salvaged and attached to a new doubletree. Dad's driving force to repair symbolized the times.

In the post-depression era of the 40s and 50s, a farmer, logger, pulpwood cutter, or any manual laborer depended greatly on the long-life use of a tool for his livelihood. Dad's scrap pile, a true mess of beyond repair junk, grew very slowly and infrequently. He held tenaciously to the attitude "keep on fixing to keep on working to make it through the hard times."

Then one day my bubble burst. While playing—helping Mom fix lunch—I dropped an egg on the floor. The mess kicked in my standing impression, and according to Mama I said, "Daddy will fix it when he gets home." My Spic'n Span Porch Mama replied, "OK" and left the egg yolk intact on the floor. Later I would understand her wisdom.

Hearing Dad coming up the back steps, I ran out on the back porch and holding onto my confidence alerted him to his next repair job. A grin broke through his coal smoked face. He scratched his chin in the usual "big Milton" way, cradled my shoulder in his big strong hand, and brought me to a new point of his limitation. "Son, thanks for waiting for me to come home. Thanks for believing what I can do, but nobody can repair a broken egg." Then he quoted the text, "Humpty Dumpty sat on a wall, Humpty Dumpty had a great fall. All the king's horses and all the king's men couldn't put Humpty Dumpty together again." Next, amidst my tears, his hugs, water, and rags (pre-paper towel days), he, Mom, and I cleaned up the floor and dropped the egg mess into the slop bucket. I cannot recall the incident damaging my above-human perception of my father. And, I believe I know why. That's the rest of this story.

Sometime later, maybe a week or even months later, Mr. Cush crept down the alley toward Dad's shop driving his old black Dodge flatbed truck. Dad and I walked out and immediately saw his big trouble—pieces, yes pieces, of a wagon tied down on the truck. Cutting right to the issue of cause and effect, and not very happy, the old man spoke, "Milton, my mules spooked, ran away from me, and then tried to run away from each other while still in the traces." Typically true to his nature, Dad asked, "How are the mules?" Deleting verbiage beyond needed usage to a 10 year-old, I concluded both jacks would work again another day. Now the big boy question, "Porch, can you put it back together?" At this point I offer a bit of explanation. In those days, and more so now, wheel hubs and metal fittings on a wagon were getting more difficult to obtain, and they were very expensive. The Pelahatchie blacksmith walked around the truck bed, shaking pieces and examining the damage. Two wheels had been shattered, leaving only broken spokes, hubs and iron tires. The front axle sustained a crack from end to end, the coupling pole had snapped, one thimble completely twisted off the rear axle lay on the floor of the truck, and the doubletree had snapped at the tongue, probably when the mules parted company. Now in the quietness following my metallurgical engineer father's inspection, I saw a bunch of *junk*. He saw, well evidently, he envisioned, an intact, ready to roll, functioning farm implement following days of hard work.

Mr. Cush offered observations, suggestions, and a series of how-tos. Knowing my Daddy, I knew it was time for Mr. Cush to leave. And Dad spoke, "Cush, you leave it here and I'll see what I can do." Intriguing answer, carefully phrased response, reality-based assessment, non-contractual understanding? In Mississippi terms—"Don't get your hopes up...yet." Omitting the long repair process (another Paw Paw Letter), weeks later

Dad and I put the finishing touches on brother Cush's fully restored Studebaker wagon—a coat of fire engine red paint. Casually touching up a few spots, Mr. Milton mused, "I wonder what the mules will think?"

As a kid, I had participated and experienced a transition from brokenness to wholeness. Of course, I could not express the change in such words as a 10 year-old. Nevertheless, I must have caught the principal. Today Aaron, your Paw Paw knows by many experiences the path from brokenness to wholeness, greatly because of my early life in a time when such process was so evident and necessary. I write this letter as a testimony to the reality—life and lives do encounter brokenness, and wholeness comes on the other side of going through struggle, hard work, and the blessing from the belief that Almighty God in Christ brings us through.

Passing on values with hope,

Paw Paw

A Simple Loss, Night Sounds

Rehoboth Hill
Cane Ridge, TN

Dear Aaron,

Once upon a time…

Sorry, no fable, so I'll begin again.

So, once upon a time in a real time during my childhood, each season extending from the warming of spring to the cooling of late fall, folks shared in the value of night sounds. I speak of a time before air conditioning and television—the era of open windows and night sitting sessions in yards and on porches, exposed to a variety of unusual symphonies, sudden noises, and mystery sounds defying recognition. These nightly entertainments began during the crowding in of darkness and continued on toward bedtime, unaltered by window screens or latched screen doors adjacent to open wood doors.

Far to the west or northwest of our house, a low growling roll of thunder usually preceded the stirring of the tall pine trees on the Methodist church property across our road. As the wind sound rose and began rushing past, we awaited the smell of coming drops of water, soon followed by downpours of rain clinking on the tin roof. Such sounds even sang me to sleep better, except for the infancy years when my mama hummed hymns to the timing of a creaking rocker.

To the older folks, the sound of such a wind and rain process gave rise to the expression, "It's going to come up a fresh."

On dry nights in between showers, the crickets and mosquitoes kept up a constant announcement of their presence. No real outdoor southern summertime experience could be enjoyed without the accompaniment of a Black Flagg mosquito sprayer. Just about bedtime, my father paraded through our house seeking out any uninvited mosquito while pumping the sprayer emitting a fine fog, filling nostrils with the combined smell of diesel fuel, coal oil, and insecticide. It worked! No self-respecting mosquito dared to fly through such a cloud and hoped to live to tell of his adventure.

Back outside, April through October, a critter combination of frogs, whippoorwills, and bob-whites blended their persistent natural audio talents to break the quietness and peace of the otherwise still night.

That trio of solos by God-made creatures, though absent from my ears for decades, still echo in my memory to take me back to an era filled with imagination and wonder about sounds from unseen sources.

Mom, Dad, and I spent numerous evenings in the pleasantry of porch sitting. Dad would somehow fold up in the swing, mama brought out her favorite ice cream table chair, and I sat on the floor of the porch, hanging my feet off but not far down enough to tempt the "boogers" waiting under the open tiered house to snatch me into their dark chasm. Boogers made noise also. As an old wood house cools off at night, intermittent creaks and groans invade the silence.

Hoot owls always frightened me. Each maintained no routine of timing or place to hoot. As a distanced hoot grew louder, I knew the feathered predator perched in some tree would soon begin ranging to begin hunting, often spying out our chicken house. Late in the night, his loud hoots would awaken me with a fright, displacing my sleep for hours.

Night time also featured folk-made sounds. A train, coal burning choo-choo and later roaring diesel, split the night into sections of time. We went to bed after the 9:00 p.m. Illinois Central westbound switched paper wood cars and passed through town. Occasionally a car passed the house, kicking up dust, and conversation immediately changed to, "Who was that?" Nighttime summer heat could also determine the length of our outside time. The bedrooms featured 12 foot ceilings, so designed for summer heat to rise. Yet the tall structures never proved to be effective, only trapping the heat.

Then one night sometime in the mid-1950s, we opted to abandon night sounds to go glare into the eye of the video display on Channels 3, 12, and 25. Gradually, the tube worked a mesmerizing effect, and nighttime became dominated by CBS, ABC, and NBC.

Tragically, our loss of night sounds prompted little accompanying grief. Our immediate around-the-house place succumbed to the effect of an artificial world begging to be seen.

For years, the outside home drama followed no script, stirred imagination, and prompted relaxation and solitude. In the transition to the TV room a few feet from the front porch, we traveled a long distance to replace God-created outside sounds to enjoy the comfort of entertainment. Folks all over town fell victim to the same allurement and simple nighttime sessions of sitting, talking, and listening while outside lost out to a desire to cloister away in house boxes up and down the streets. And even more tragically, such was the beginning of the end of neighborhoods of a long time ago.

Passing on values with hope,

Paw Paw

Thank God, Mama Tried

Rehoboth Hill
Cane Ridge, TN

Dear Aaron,

Mama, Miss Lillian, Sister Porch, Sweet Mom—four identity relationships only now known as part of "the great cloud of witnesses" (Hebrews 12:1). Lillian Olivia Barnes, daughter of Jim and Bessie Barnes, first drew breath November 24, 1910 in a small log house in the Barefoot Springs community of Rankin County. Her mother's close friend, Rosie Edwards, attended Lillian's birth and placed girl number four in my Grandmother Bessie's arms. A hard life among ten siblings developed her resiliency to sustain her for 87 years. Each of the Father's created persons defies any definition, and rightly so, and especially my dear mother. She by no doubt of her own peers played out her lead role in her own life drama. Tough enough to survive, tender enough to surrender to the call to nursing, and all her in-between antics, trials, politics, ministries, affections, and resistances contributed to her fulfillment of being totally herself.

She began nursing school in the old Mississippi state asylum upon the dawn of The Great Depression. Her schooling, she chose to interrupt after her father broke his leg turning over a bale of cotton one Sunday morning, and demanded Lillian the nurse must "come home to take care of me." She never surrendered the dream and returned to school 36 years later, and practiced nursing until her retirement after the age 80.

She and Dad married on Easter Sunday 1935 when she was 25 and he was 47.

Wife Lillian moved into Dad's house—a most basic bachelor pad desperately in need of a woman's loving touch. She attacked first the closets and their accompanying junk. Opening the first one, she spied a long black thing hanging down. Slamming the door, she grabbed a hoe near the back door, ran back to the closet, cracked the door open and attacked the snake-appearing object, now realizing she had cut her husband's best black belt into two equal pieces. For some odd reason, this story often repeated always stopped at that point.

After losing twins, she gave me birth and consciously wrapped my life around the character of the boy Samuel. The ever intermittent expanding dimensions of my Christian life began through her discipline in local Baptist church life. I grew up scheduled by Sunday school, BTU, Sunbeams, worship service, prayer meetings, and all other open-the-door church events.

Dad died a few days after their 25th wedding anniversary. As an 18-year-old boy, I observed her grief and began to catch the depth of the bond of her love for him. Only after her death, to borrow from George Jones, "She stopped lovin' him today." They made marriage work, and along the way her witness led him to accept Christ as his Savior.

Our house sat on a series of brick, concrete, and wood tiers strategically placed to provide the foundation. Our area of Mississippi included a soil type unaffectionately called "Yazoo clay"—sponge-like dirt subject to moving according to the rise and fall of moisture. Therefore, the foundation shifted, resulting in doors dragging or failing to close. The bathroom door seemed to hang and drag more often than any other door. Mama had this thing about visiting company and a bathroom door that would not close tight. So Dad placed house jacks, heavy screw-type greasy iron stanchions under beams to offset the drag on the doors. Occasionally due to my childhood delicate size, Mama, overly perplexed by a stubborn door, sent me under the house to move and reset a jack, thereby facilitating opening and closing of a hung up door. Once I was under the house expecting to be swallowed at any moment by a giant snake or booger, she would shout down directions aiming me to the dragging spot. Jacks in place, I slowly began rotating the big screw to the creaking sound of a long leaf pine timber while awaiting her call, "Enough!" Crawling back out took minimal time compared to the crawl toward the ailing spot.

An invitation to be inducted into the Mary Frances Chapter # 222 of the Order of the Eastern Star carried the recognition of high class honor of our local community culture. Candidates underwent rigorous review as to character, habits, and lineage. Our Baptist pastor applied. A committee discovered an unpaid bill during a previous pastorate. His rejection by the Order of the Eastern Star prompted his forced termination by the church. They took that stuff seriously.

Well, Miss Lillian made the cut. She got in and went, as said in the south, "hog wild." Eastern Star consumed my Mama. Daddy had a cynical side. He overworked his affliction poking fun at Mama. Actually, anything short of manual labor appeared silly to him.

Mama kept her fraternal stuff—papers, schedules, and ritual book in one special "stay out" but unlocked drawer. At the outset of her Eastern Star season, she lectured me on the hazards of opening that drawer. Progressing through late childhood, bordering on rebellious adolescence, one day I gave in to the devil and quietly pulled open the drawer. As far back as I recall, closed books have attracted me. There in the center of the holy drawer, positioned carefully at right angle and equally distant from all sides of the cubicle, lay the pale tan hard bound gold lettered cover off-limits book. As curiosity slid into intrigue and to the beat of my heavy pounding heart, I lifted the volume out and quickly began turning pages, mystified by strange charts, weird signs, scary symbols, and a growing fear of desecration. I knew I returned her ritual book to its exact honored position. Days later, in her interrogative/suspicious manner, Mama asked me, "Did you open my Eastern Star drawer?" My confession led to warnings bordering on terror.

My intrigue faded. Today, over a decade after her death, I have the little book. I've never opened it again. I never will. Silly? Oh, no! Respect extends beyond one's life.

Mama moved up through the Order and became Worthy Matron. Obsession kicked in as she lived out in Eastern Star terms her "year in the East." The Worthy Matron sits in the chair on the Eastern side of the room. I had to attend the non-secret part of her induction, coronation, inauguration, ordination, or whatever. A few other times I sat outside waiting for the meeting to end. All doors into the chapter room had round holes covered over with larger round pieces of wood that if moved one could peep in and watch the proceedings. Not me! That room on second floor of our city hall occupied space directly over the cells of the town jail. Remember, a kid my age still an elementary Baptist under the burden of a regular dose of guilt preaching knew about the horror of being zapped.

Along about half way through the Worthy Matron year as Mama left the house one evening for an OES meeting, Daddy asked me, "Son, do you think we'll survive your Mama's year in the East?" We did!

Sister Porch's childhood duties included washing clothes around a boiling black pot and rub board. Sometime in the late 30s, despite The Great Depression, Daddy upgraded the home with the purchase of a Kenmore wringer washer.

Early in the 1950's a mechanical marvel, the Bendix Automatic washing machine, revolutionized American home laundry. Mama, who extended her Eastern Star-like determination, set out to own the first Bendix in town. Dad and Mama's response to progress traveled at very different speeds. Besides, the Kenmore worked well after 20 years of service. Over time, selling a few pies and cakes, substituting in the school lunchroom, holding back a little grocery money, she saved up the down payment, bought the new washer, and committed herself to an unheard of venture in our house—the demon, credit. Upon delivery and following orientation to hazardous duties in installing the Bendix, the dearly beloved textbook married couple Lillian and Milton of tree lined shady Munsterman dirt road had an issue—never physical but highly vocal, highly emotional, and rarely rational, and then mutual solitude set in for days. Finally, stupidity resolved as Daddy took savings and paid off the Bendix. Years later, I heard the other side of the story. When Mama told him she planned to pay off the appliance by taking in washing, he lost his cool, "_____ _____, my wife will never take in washing." She had splattered his dignity all over the floor. A plot? Don't think so. Conniving never made her fault list.

And the Bendix story goes on. Finally Dad, with my reluctant help, crawled under the house and bolted the washer down. This preceded the days when vibrating automatic washers could stand alone. Dad, a limited electrician who identified a hot wire by touch, rigged an electric line out of a screw-in fuse box to supply current to the appliance, and Mama planned a party to show off Pelahatchie's first Bendix automatic washer. She invited the Timothy, Eunice, Lois, and the Ready Sunday School classes of the Baptist church, the Order of the Eastern Star ladies, and the Methodist mission ladies. They gathered in our kitchen on the appointed day. Mama explained the features of the machine and began the process of washing some already clean towels. Those old automatics laundered clothes through soak, wash, rinse, and spin cycles. Oh, the delight filling the room until the spin/wringer cycle kicked in. Rapid centrifugal force snapped all bolts off, and the spinning washer went dancing across the kitchen to the cries and screams of the town's elite ladies. Party's over! The following week Daddy bolted it down to the floor on the back porch. His concluding remark—"Now go dance out in the yard."

Around town, most folks understood in various degrees of amusement how Mama put her design on my future vocation. In all honesty and with sincere appreciation, she did subject me to options. In review, I recall three movements—the arts, medicine, and ministry. All along I supplied various and intermittent degrees of cooperation, both subtle and overt.

Oh, the arts! Piano lessons, vocal studies, elocution, and as difficult as it is to admit—three ballet lessons. Only piano offered any hope, and that came only upon being dismissed by a teacher heavy on techniques and being welcomed by the Baptist church pianist who recognized my gift would never reach beyond *The Broadman Hymnal*. I fought the voice lessons! Her patience extended to a deal, "You take a 30 minute voice lesson and I'll buy you a ticket to the Lamar or Paramount movie theater. Her steady work as a nurse paid for the lessons and my bargaining. The voice lessons, while an endurance, offered me the opportunities to see movies I still remember, including "The Pride of St. Louis," "Battle Cry," "Them" (giant ants), "Thunder Road," and "Oklahoma."

The medical direction began with her observation that my small hands would easily adapt to surgery. At her insistence, I learned some basic first-aid, and it has been a life blessing. Once nurse Porch connected my throwing up to seeing road kill, the medical profession alert leveled off.

Sometimes, mamas call children into Christian ministry. My Mama did not call me. Years after surrendering to my calling, I intentionally analyzed the big picture of my call with a trusted friend over a period of time. I know God gave her a role in my spiritual development. Regardless of other folk's perception, I understand and cherish her folded hands wrapped around mine teaching me, "Now I lay me down to sleep." The Good Friday afternoon that she, while ironing, bore verbal witness of Christ to me, lives daily with me. I easily visualize our times huddled close to a natural gas heater on January nights as I struggled to memorize the first twelve chapters of John for the Bible memorization contest. Somewhere a box of my memory stuff of her includes a little red book entitled *Samuel, the Temple Boy.* Only minimal effort sends me back to hear her inflection, "Samuel, Samuel." She periodically increased my repertoire of Scripture by focus on passages such as John 3:16, Psalm 1, Psalm 23, II Chronicles 7:14, Romans 3:23, and the basis for all Scripture, II Timothy 3:16. I settled at age eight by her help an issue to afflict so many in decades later, especially the multitude who could never grasp the simple truth of the authority of Scripture as declared by Scripture.

Call my partial review as you see fit. For me, I got good mama-ing while being raised right.

Passing on values with hope,

Paw Paw

Blacksmith Shop Work Ethics

Rehoboth Hill
Cane Ridge, TN

Dear Aaron,

Once in a season past, the five Porch boys (my Dad, Milton, and his four brothers, sons of John Jackson and Martha Eleanor Porch) all surrendered to the noble calling of blacksmithing. Their era proved to be the last generation of men making a living by horrid heat, heavy hammers, and hard hits on an anvil.

My numerous blessings of being raised right in the South included daily play and/or work, six days a week, from age four to eighteen alongside a master teacher, a tutor of practical hard work. In addition to moving through the grades of a town local school, I served out a family apprenticeship to the town's best sage of wisdom in the midst of black, oily smut and coal smoke. These previous sentences offer conclusions. During my years in the shop receiving no pay, but rather contributing to the family welfare, admittedly I often wanted to be somewhere else to play with other boys or receive my freedom from the shop. Still, through adequate time spent with Big Milton, I today value his gift to me much more than any diploma or degree.

The shop intentionally provoked the absence of signs of success while it assuredly advertised efficiency. No diplomas, no writs of certification hung conspicuously near the open door. No dusty glass frame surrounded a grade displayed from the periodic visit of a state approved blacksmithologist.

Rather, the quality of his work was recognized back on the farm, along logging trails and in repairs to county roads. Dad's labor represented a junction point. Work well done in the tin-topped shop enabled labor to proceed out yonder through hands making a living for families.

So, as best I can recall, Dad first connected me to his work by surrendering to my persistence to turn the blower to the forge. A reliable coal fire in a blacksmith shop requires a steady, consistent flow of air. The Champion blower's effect depended on the rhythmic not-too-fast, not-too-slow revolutions of the blower handle. Erratic airflow could result in overheating or retarding the heat process, thereby wasting time. Over my experiences, probably months, in Dad's words, "Son, you got it about right." That often spoken term now reminds me some life qualities often reside in environments wherein I know I have not perfected by endeavors of ministry for Christ.

In time I moved up to the frustrating assignment of taking apart old rusty plows, cracked Pittman rods, big mud covered splintered single trees, and busted road-worn wagon wheels. By no stretch of imagination could my energies expended through crescent wrenches, pliers, cold chisels, hammers, and heavy grease (resulting in skinned knuckles and torn fingernails) ever be categorized as works of art. In Dad's mind, the jobs fit my ability. Besides, frustration nearing the urge of expletives premiered the reality of struggle, yet a personal lifelong accompaniment.

Again, to the best of my remembering, my first constructive solo job assignment involved the process of making bridge pins. These two-foot pieces of steel resembled gigantic headless nails that, once driven into heavy oak timbers, literally held bridges together over streams and creeks on county gravel roads. I began by cutting a long section of re-bar into two foot sections with a hammer and anvil cleaver. Next, after heating one end of the pin, I sharpened the red hot metal into a point. Following air cooling, the pin could easily be driven into the bridge timber. It was a simple process, but more so to a young boy, a sense of accomplishment.

Saturday, come-to-town day in an agrarian area, was Dad's busiest and longest day of the week; most shop activity required constant use of the forge. Dozens of plow points—middle busters, buzzard wing sweeps, half shovels, harrow pins, and walking cultivator tips—all needed the blacksmith's careful sharpening skills. Sometimes six or eight plow points would lie on or in the fire, requiring careful watching to prevent overheating or neglect in the heating sequence. The number of irons in the fire could exceed time needed to attend to each one. Each tool had to be struck by a hammer when the heat reached the point that the metal was malleable.

And so the dual truth—"too many irons in the fire at the same time" and "you strike when the iron is hot."

No process intrigued me more in the blacksmith shop, and no process exceeded my young skills more, than the master art of horseshoeing. Cleaning and properly shaping the hooves initiated the delicate operation. Improper hoof cleaning resulting in careless nail driving could injure, even lame, a horse. Dad revered animals and tolerated no abuse around his shop. A later letter will detail this claim. Once Dad cleaned and trimmed the hoof, he laid a new shoe on each foot. He possessed an amazing perception to recall how to shape each shoe in the setting up process.

New shoes out of a keg all looked the same. Thus, each horseshoe required some shoe reshaping over his anvil, and one by one he shaped each red hot shoe. Once shaped to his satisfaction, the shoes went into the slack tub for cooling. Thrown on the ground for final cooling, a cold looking shoe could still badly burn a boy's foot. One deep burn one day and I gained total respect to an even cold looking horseshoe.

Dad wore a heavy leather apron to protect his legs while holding the hoof to nail on the shoes. A first time shod or skittish horse sometimes opted not to cooperate. Out came the nose twister—a two foot, graduated to a point wood stick with a rope looped through a hole at the big end. A hand full of horse nose went in the loop, and after twisting the loop taut, the snorting animal usually quieted down. Dad often awarded me the job of holding the twister and gently rubbing the nose—a dangerous act performed under the caution, "If he rears up, let him go." Why? Horses don't always hurt people with back legs. Looking back, I remember seeing well set shoes, properly nailed tight and bonded, and dressed off with a hoof rasp, a work of art.

Filling a wagon wheel always promised to be our most enjoyable joint work. Usually, farmers brought in the remains of a broken wheel—splintered spokes, rotten rims, or a loose fitting tire. The challenge was to fill the wheel from the hub out. The hub, quite expensive, seldom required replacement, provided the broken spokes were carefully removed. Over the years, I improved my skills with a hammer and wood chisel, and if I do say so, mastered the art of cleaning up a hub. The actual filling the wheel process could require a half a day in time, depending on interruptions. The multistep process included driving in new spokes, shaving and shaping spoke ends, affixing the circular wood rim followed by heating and shrinking the steel tire to the wood rim, plus finally bolting the tire to the rim. A correctly filled wagon wheel, once finished, conveys a dish look. On a wagon, a wheel rolled dishing out from the axle to enhance balance and prevent binding. To my father, the appearance of the dish effect determined the degree of his satisfaction with the job. Occasionally, at intervals in the process, he repeated steps in improving the dish look, thereby insuring a properly constructed wheel.

As I write, details of the wheel process fill my mind. The last time my father and I worked together, we filled a wheel. A few days later, I left for college. Dad suffered a massive heart attack in the late fall and never returned to his shop.

As an only child of a 54-year-old father, I came along at the right time to fall heir to his wisdom. This observation endears me more to the Biblical prophet, Jeremiah.

Dad, a son of a sharecropper and one of seven siblings, shared in an integrity and satisfying identity of being one of the Porches. No mystery cloaked this work ethic. Each boy caught the quality as a gift borne of hard manual labor.

Big Milton, the blacksmith, outlasted four local competitors, a testament to his labor. He worked with an urgency tempered by quality and awareness that his work's real test would be made back on the farm or in the woods. Frequently, he faced a mess, an implement to me shattered beyond repair but needed by a struggling farmer. He'd scratch his whiskered chin and affirm the hope of, "Let me see what I can do." A day or so later, he returned to the broken plow or seemingly worn out tool. Now, mind work completed, he had a plan to guide his energy and the intention to aid a friend/customer to finish out a crop year.

After Dad died (1960), Mom and I began the long process of choices—tools to keep, some to sell, and the frustrating disposition of Mr. Milton's sacred scrap pile, source of many remedies for what seemed beyond repair.

The grief stage included a review of his simple credit account book managed by Mom. They referred to the ledger as "I'll pay you when my crop comes in." Many folk apparently never brought in a crop. Yet, Dad never dunned

31

(demanded payment) of anyone except the county. Now over half a century later, I've caught his greatest lesson yet. In my words, quality hard work offers personal joy. I believe he ministered through his well done labor and bore testimony to his Heavenly Father.

Passing on values with hope,

Paw Paw

Church Home, Always Local

Rehoboth Hill
Cane Ridge, TN

Dear Aaron,

Pardon me, Aaron, only now has Paw Paw's consciousness gotten around to amusing you by reminiscing and narrating some quite unique and personal happenings through the ministry of my church family in our small Baptist church. Oh, I know, the local church belongs to Jesus. But please, for this letter, grant me the honor to refer to my church—a most endearing term then and now.

As best I remember, I was four or five years old. One summer afternoon, an older teenager accepted the responsibility to take care of the children during the weekly Woman's Missionary Union meeting. Probably, this new venture had not been carefully considered for our age or maximum safety. She began, "Boys and girls, our game today will be spin the bottle. First let's find a bottle." The diligent search around the church resulted only in a discarded, nasty, glass Double Cola bottle with a broken lip and sharp edge. She pronounced the find "perfect" for the game. So each child, wearing shorts, gathered in a circle and crossed his or her legs. The object of the game focused on each person spinning the bottle and eliminating someone according to the way the bottle pointed at the end of the rotation. Upon my turn, I gave the glass weapon a hearty spin, and the bottle spun toward me and cut a two inch gash across my knee. Blood, real red blood spurting out, kids crying, squalling, big-time medical alert, mamas running out of the WMU meeting, neighbors hollering, frantic searching for the pastor, cars driving by screeching to a stop, everyone deserting me sitting bleeding and waiting for the pain to set in. Wow, what attention! I wish now I had thought up a good faint. Oh, well, in minutes, tragedy averted and Rev. George Washington Smith carried me next door to Dr. Johnson's house clinic, all the way listening to my nurse mama's diagnosis and treatment plan. Today a faint scar remains as a constant bodily effective warning, daring me to never spin the bottle again.

During his pastoral tenure, the Rev. J. F. S. caught a vision for a Royal Ambassador softball team. Three of us gathered too early for practice the first day and quickly grew tired of waiting on the steps near the pastor's study. Unwisely, we began batting practice between the church sanctuary and parsonage, a narrow area about 30 feet wide. Intending to be very careful, I pitched slowly and S. tried to just tap the ball. He did—right through a large opaque sanctuary window, shattering the entire sash. Immediate awareness! Big-time church trouble.

Later that beautiful summer afternoon, S.'s mama visited my mother for a sisters of the church mature Christian discussion regarding just and equitable distribution of cost to replace the window so desecrated by their sons. One of their major issues centered around blame and fault. The two gracious mothers held strongly to different opinions. S.'s mama built a case for equal sin by both boys. My mama adequately defended me as having no intention of breaking a church window. According to Mama, S. had three options, "Miss the ball, swing not at the ball, or hit the ball." His choice to hit the ball, in Mama's opinion, exonerated her precious boy. Following that episode, I became a careful student of my mother's logic. Oh, yes, the two old girls finally settled on sharing the cost. My father's narration would not be appropriate in this letter.

The next story, credible to a mass of witnesses, will require extra tact to survive censorship.

Once again, the WMU brought upon me great misery. A committee of five ladies, my mama, her two sisters, and two other protected ladies, accepted the awesome challenge to present a theme interpretation on The Fruits of the Spirit during the summer Rankin County associational WMU conclave. By summer, I mean big-time July hot summer in the non-air conditioned Briar Hill Baptist Church. The committee arrived upon the conclusion to creatively involve the Sunbeams (forerunner of Mission Friends) in the presentation.

For several weeks each Monday afternoon, each Sunbeam practiced his or her lines or memory verse, all related to the biblical teaching of The Fruits of the Spirit.

Unknown to any of us, clandestinely the big five mamas had sewn crepe paper costumes of various colors to resemble fruits—red apple, pink grapefruit, purple grape, yellow banana, green pear, orange orange, and so forth—a different color for each child.

The big day arrived. Our Sunbeam caravan traveled all the way to the Briar Hill Baptist Church. We arrived just in time for lunch—pimento cheese sandwiches, fried chicken, and gallons of cold sweet tea. After the hurried lunch and refills on tea, the boys and two mamas went down one path, and the girls and three mamas took a path in the opposite direction, each path leading to the "facility."

Once back in the church house, boys and girls went again in opposite directions to selected rooms. Now, here's where this story really gets tricky. We boys were told to strip down to our underwear. Remember, the mid 1940's offered little resemblance to the world of today. Each boy assumed the same instructions were given to the girls. At that time, the mama matrons brought out the costumes.

Surprise! As each boy realized what was in the making, pure frustration, shame, and only the good Lord knows what began to take over. Nevertheless, our male resistance gradually melted into obedience by way of maternal threats, in Christian guilt terms. Once suited up, legs and arms sticking out of the gaudy, shapeless apparel, we filed out to meet the equally embarrassed girls.

Now remember, July heat inside a Baptist church in the South rises through the day. By now, after 1:00 p.m., our Sunbeam perspiration had turned to Baptist sweat. Crepe paper, like puckered nylon, does not breathe like cotton cloth. Crepe paper holds in heat. Heat in crepe paper on a body produces more sweat. The sweat and crepe paper began rubbing together. The moisture, once in contact with crepe paper, washed out the color. Now colored sweat dripped off each precious body, every drop puddling around the tightly sewn seams gathered around both legs. Apparently, any moisture over maybe a half pint exceeded each costume's capacity. So we marched out on the podium of the Briar Hill Baptist Church just as each costume began leaking. Very soon, rivulets of color began traveling down each leg. Some of the congregation applauded the feature as planned creative effects. Worst of all, one boy with mixed anxiety and embarrassment forgot his lines and proved his consumption of tea exceeded the production of his trip to the facility. Overall, my Sunbeam companions and I that day came face to face with disaster at an early age.

Once I became 13, I qualified for the older boys' Sunday School class. The previous summer, a young seminary student from our church returned home awaiting a call to a pastorate. In the meantime, he accepted the opportunity to teach the boys' class. Intending to begin with a "get to know you" fellowship for each member of the class, he announced his first Sunday that the following Friday night he would host a peanut boiling. Let me explain the Southern tradition. Green peanuts, freshly dug out of the ground, are carefully washed off and then boiled in a rolling salt brine until they are tender. These delicacies are best eaten when they are hot. The group traveled out to a nearby lake, built a roaring fire, and placed the pot of green peanuts filled with salt water on the fire. Sometime later, once the peanuts were tender, we began the process of gluttony. Later that evening, all peanuts having been consumed, our teacher announced he would take us to Morton eight miles away for chocolate milkshakes. He owned a fairly new automobile. Nine boys and their teacher, tummies bulging with green peanuts, consumed a large chocolate milkshake from Gunn's Dairy Bar. Approximately half way between Morton and our home town, the highway passes through a large chicken farm. The combination of fresh boiled peanuts, over-chocolated milkshake, and the ambiance of the chicken houses touched off a disaster similar to that affliction Jonah suffered following his days and nights in the fish. Each boy contributed to the mess. The following Sabbath, we assembled for Sunday School and met a new teacher. Apparently the seminary student deserted youth ministry. Within a few months, he became an Air Force chaplain.

I do not know for sure, but I don't believe kids today can have such momentous experiences as those afforded in my home church. To say ministry is to stretch the term quite far. Looking back a long, long way, I am thankful for memories that can be enjoyed at a time distance.

Passing on values with hope,

Paw Paw

Once a Bubba, Maybe Always

Rehoboth Hill
Cane Ridge, TN

Dear Aaron,

Mamma tried!

Oh my, how my Mamma tried to give me greater appreciation for the fine arts of culture.

Overall, I lived through four phases of lessons in ballet, diction, piano, and voice. You've read the ballet story. As to diction, there's not much to tell—just a funny fellow named Fred who talked through his nose.

The big story is in the music. Our town featured a musical division between the piano students of Mrs. M. and Mrs. G. You either resided in one camp or the other.

Around the ripe age of nine, Mamma embarked on my musical career. Bearing the conviction of my hidden talent, she went to the big city of Jackson, bought newspapers, found pianos for sale in the want ads, bought one, and went back home to announce to my Daddy, "Milton, I bought a piano so James can take lessons." Even a nine year-old knows the look of marital stress. As it turned out, Daddy's biggest concern was underpinning the living room floor to prevent sagging from the weight of the old upright instrument.

Nevertheless, in the interest of "culture," Daddy crawled under the house and built support beams to bear the weight of the out-of-tune giant delivered to the house by my uncle who worked for a moving company.

Mamma enrolled me in the G. Academy of the Piano. Mrs. G's lessons were only 50 cents—10 cents cheaper than Mrs. M's lessons.

Armed with John Thompson's *Teaching Little Fingers to Play*, I faithfully arrived at 3:30 p.m. on a Tuesday. For the next eight years, I gave all Tuesdays and Friday afternoons from 3:30-4:00 p.m. to the study of the piano. To put the subject mildly, Mrs. G and I did <u>not</u> begin with rapport, never developed mutual appreciation and, as far as I know, I was the only piano student she ever fired.

Now along the way, there were some better moments, but I never could curve my fingers to suit her and I cringed at her beating time with a long knitting needle. Still, the process continued as I learned to play a few hymns. Prior to the piano lessons, my musical exposure only included singing hymns at church, listening to the Grand Old Opry belching country music from an old Philco Cathedral radio, and one song taught to me by my father. The words included, "The old cow died in the fork of the branch, the jay bird whistled, and the buzzard danced."

After adding a few hymns to my repertoire, Mamma began her campaign to work me in to the Sunday night church piano accompaniment rotation. Big mistake! The M students controlled that worship spot and had maintained the monopoly for years.

Nevertheless, Mamma prevailed on Rev. Stanford to alter the usual routine to include guess who. In respect to my limited repertoire, our song leader chose the same songs each occasion I laboriously played for church.

In a short time, the more accomplished M students took over the Hammond organ on Sunday night. Guess again. I moved up to organist, mainly through Mamma's church politics. Through these performances, Sunday night church took on a different meaning for me, usually affected by my multiple digestive afflictions—some even unknown to medical science. I was awful. Attendance dropped, and Daddy even boycotted my playing. He suddenly invoked the Sabbath evening as rest time for the coming week.

Finally, with little or no regard, Mrs. G notified Mamma she had terminated my lessons. Feigning public disappointment and yet holding happiness inside, I experienced liberation. Short lived! Mamma moved immediately to consult with Mrs. M by pleading my case with her passion about my yet-to-be-discovered or appreciated talents. This happened during the summer after my 11th grade year. I believe only by her graciousness did Mrs. M take

me on, confident she could endure my limited musical development for
at least one year.

Now, allow me to interrupt the flow for a point of defense. I liked music.
I did not enjoy practicing and avoided the discipline of scales, theories,
and key identifications, and I could never remember the meaning of
those music symbols. Actually, I liked playing hymns but resisted the
learning process. My senior year, Mrs. M basically focused me on hymns,
an appreciation I hold to this day. I really think my high school diploma
should have read "High School Graduate *Cum Hymn.*"

Meanwhile during the piano odyssey, I experienced another adventure
in Mamma's quest to develop my vocal talent. By the way, by now Dad's
Social Security and World War I service-connected disability pension had
kicked in, and financially the family was on the rise.

One Saturday shortly after my 12th birthday, Mamma and I rode to Jackson
in our 1951 Cambridge teal green Plymouth. She parked in front of an old
house behind Sears and announced, "Here's where we are going to take
voice lessons." "What do you mean 'we'?" "We" really meant "me." We
walked into Frank Slater's studio over against my tears and pleading and
Mamma's assurance, "One day you'll thank me."

For three years, Mr. Slater bore up under my disinterest and refusal to
practice. He coached, fussed, worked on my guilt, screamed, and even
threw up his hands.

One Saturday another student, a young girl named Julia, completed her
lesson just ahead of me and Mr. Slater came out of the studio praising
her for a good lesson. Julia's mom casually replied, "Oh, that's due to
all the spaghetti and meatballs she ate for lunch." You guessed it. Each
Saturday from then on, I had spaghetti and meatballs for lunch—all good
intentioned by Mamma in hope of my musical progress.

At the same point in my voice studies, Mamma overheard Mr. Slater talking
with another student encouraging him to audition for the Vienna Boys
Choir. Auditions were scheduled following their concert at the Jackson
City Auditorium. Fearful, I checked a world map in search of Vienna. I
discovered the place, a city in Austria next to Germany and nearby Russia.
Now the anxiety reached a new height.

Well, the concert featured a big bunch of little boys in blue coats, knee britches and long socks, singing in high-pitched screeches, gesturing with outstretched palms-up hands. I concluded somehow, no way was this boy getting on the boat to Vienna with that bunch of sissies!

The next sad event probably saved me from world travel.

By now, Dad, very limited in reading, subscribed for the *Jackson Daily News*, a state newspaper. A few weeks following the Vienna screech fest, the paper featured on the front page an announcement, "Renowned Episcopalian Choir Master Frank Slater Dies Unexpectedly." Immediately, both grief and relief warred inside me and, quite honestly, relief won. I never heard about the Vienna Boys Choir again and figured my voice venture a closed book.

Wrong again!

Mamma just moved on down North State Street to the Studio of Charles McCool, Lessons in Piano and Voice. He subscribed to a single purpose—show-casing his students in recitals. For six months, each Saturday morning at 10:00 a.m., he and I (mostly he) focused on an Irish ditty, *The Rose of Tralee*. Trying to learn that song a few hours after you've slopped hogs or spent hours hoeing corn, taxes one with accelerated stress. Mamma maintained her persistence. She moved into mediation, offering me a movie ticket to either the Lamar or Paramount Theater following each peaceful and cooperative lesson. She won. I played the course and finally participated in the recital.

The humor in this letter represents no disrespect for my good and gracious Mother. Her looking ahead, believing in me even beyond my skills, and most of all her love investment planted a seed now bearing fruit in my desire to make it through hard times and finish well.

Today, Aaron, Paw Paw claims little music ability but great affection for hymns, southern gospel, the great classics, and country music. Maybe through all my resistance, lack of appreciation and even manipulation, Mamma's try really worked. Today she's one of my "cloud of witnesses." So with wet eyes looking to the eastern sky, I thank you Mamma—you tried.

Passing on values with hope,

Paw Paw

Chicken Yard Lessons Still Linger

Rehoboth Hill
Cane Ridge, TN

Dear Aaron,

This letter addresses a most serious concern—chickens. More specifically, the role of the chicken in my post-depression home. I grew up around chickens, free-range and yard birds. In reality, I liken the value of a Rhode Island Red, White Leghorn, and a Dominecker to the buffalo so essential to Native Americans in the great American west. As I have written earlier, the Great Depression era pushed folks to embrace the "make it through" challenge, and our chickens provided one of the means for persistent survival. In addition, I use a valuable lesson learned in my chicken days quite often.

Our chicken compound, composed of a fenced yard and tin roof shack, carefully located to the west of our house, respected the ambiance produced by prevailing winds. The five foot high wire fence enclosure included only one gate. The single entrance and exit spot indicated that outsiders approached a restricted area. To leave the gate open and risk escaping chickens gave credence to number eight of the seven cardinal sins. In essence, chickens merited protection and care, or "don't mess with the chickens."

The violation of the posted chicken yard resulted in one of my most disciplinary experiences.

One day, I extended the range of my cowboy and Native American activity into the chicken compound. Riding a stick horse, armed with a new cap pistol and a string whip attached to a broom handle, I attempted to herd the chickens into the hen house. Old hens cackle easily, and the mixed chorus resulted in disturbance of the chickens. Just when Mamma rushed out of the house to check on her disturbed chickens, I began my approach

41

to take on the head rooster. No rooster bows to any herd instinct. I met the feathered protector head-on. Even at the age of 10, I should have known by his body language and arrogant walk that the old boy owned the yard. He pecked, I screamed, and Mamma broke off a peach tree limb on the way to the yard. She switched my legs in the chicken yard amidst feeble attempts to dodge that rooster.

Late one night a varmint got in our chicken house. Scared chickens can awaken a whole neighborhood at night. Daddy jumped out of bed in his skimpy summer sleeping attire, grabbed his old German Luger pistol, and tore out the back door. By the light of flashlight and moon, he navigated barefooted through the chicken residual to find a big possum baying the feathered ladies. He shot and missed the possum, blowing a hole in the side of the hen house big enough for the possum to make a hasty retreat. Fortunately, no chickens suffered injury.

Now if your interest has neared the point of intrigue, allow me to explain a southern post-depression era family's chicken obsession.

Hard times narrow one's value list to essentials. The chicken provided eggs, and in that era most southern recipes included an egg or eggs. Working folks' breakfast featured eggs fried in lard or hot cakes lightened in texture by the power of a stirred in egg. An egg pie contained mostly, yep—you guessed it, eggs. Southern corn bread devoid of Yankee sugar gained digestible texture by the chemical presence of an egg. Many a sick child's recovery (including mine) often could be attributed to a daily diet of egg milk—raw eggs and sugar mixed in milk. I recall my mother pausing in the midst of her cooking, having reached the point of instruction, "Son, now get me an egg." And deviled eggs—what a delight! Dry boiled yolks mixed with homemade mayonnaise and chopped up pickle, while infrequently served, did remind us that a delicacy could exist in hard times. Now, my attention to egg cooking could go on and on, but let's save some space for the chicken, literally behind the egg.

No entrée (meat dish) exceeds southern fried chicken. All attempts to improve on this God-given process results in abuse to the creature. Most restaurant menus feature fancy names for chicken, usually just covering up or disguising the fact they can't fry a decent chicken. A pullet, or fryer, cut into two thighs, two legs, two breasts, and one pulley bone, merits the dignity of being properly battered and deep-fried, seasoned only with salt and pepper. The back, wings, and neck aren't worth the wasted grease. As a Gentile, I learned an early repulsion to chicken soup and just endured the nagging cold and fever.

My third dimension of chicken utility focuses on the feathers. All my Grandmamma Barnes' grandchildren took naps or slept nights on feather mattresses. Folks a bit higher up the economic ladder boasted of goose feathers. For my family, chicken feathers provided just another means to make do.

Earlier I mentioned the fact that chickens taught me lessons. This epistle features only one, learned through the baby chicken hatching process.

As I remember, a hatch-off began with careful selection of the hen—the mother-to-be. The importance of this fact is realized that a hen labeled with the term, "She won't set" meant chicken and dumplins real soon.

A setting of eggs—usually 12—received examination under a bright light. Any flaw, thin crack, blood spot, or split yolk invalidated that egg. The nest received fresh straw, and then the eggs were carefully placed in a tight circle and the hen lowered slowly onto the eggs. Sometimes re-sitting was required, but usually the instinct of the old mother hen prevailed and the hatching began.

The hen attended to the three essentials for hatching her eggs. She provided heat, patience in waiting, and the knowledge when to gently nudge and turn the eggs. Mamma routinely checked each nest, carefully feeling under the hen to ensure eggs had proper warmth and none had rolled outside the hatch area. All the time she kept talking quietly, touching the hen gently. Looking back, I label their mutual trust as a bond. On occasion, Mamma picked up the mother hen and caressed her as the chicken lady quietly clucked her thanks. Then one day, the right day, the baby bitties began to hatch. They emerged from their home, shells wet and full of chirp. Soon they dried to a ball of yellow fur, anxious to leave the nest.

Now, my lesson! The entire hatching process honors the principle of patient change. That process from egg to baby chick has been working since God's creation. Change, more than merely important, maintained our Heavenly Father's processes continually.

Sadly, we seek out books, articles, and attend seminars on how to change when a six-week chicken-watch could be much more beneficial. Dr. James L. Sullivan likened impatient change to folks trying to hatch an egg with a blowtorch who in the process burned down the chicken house.

Aaron, I know you abide in a world of chicken fingers, chicken nuggets, and Egg Beaters. Sadly, you may never have the opportunity to observe the hatching process of chickens. So, with that sad reality, I write to say to you, "Character includes honoring patient change."

Passing on values with hope,

Paw Paw

Life While Wonder Lived

Rehoboth Hill
Cane Ridge, TN

Dear Aaron,

Among Paw Paw's afflictions, in addition to compulsively buying shirts, is that he suffers the fine art of TV channel surfing. I've surrendered to the shirt thing as a great mystery locked in the darkest recesses of my mind. On the other hand, due time has arrived to announce the revelation of why I run the channel list. In a few words, Paw Paw grew up immensely deprived of entertainment possibilities, and apparently attempts now to make up for the lost privileges.

Now through misty eyes, occasionally blotting a tear, I shall attempt to narrate my story of the exposure to the golden age of radio, the joys of double-feature Saturday afternoon matinees, and the arrival of black and white television into metropolitan Pelahatchie. These three together, seen earlier as deprivations, are now known as blessings.

Our Philco Cathedral electric radio held five tubes and required an antenna wire affixed to the window screen. Over the years, the old set rested in various rooms of the house. Our family enjoyed the best sound once the radio found its home in front of a window in the northwest corner of the back bedroom. Quite logical! That spot placed the radio in a direct line to the radio stations in Jackson, Mississippi 25 miles away, and also faced Nashville to the north for the WSM Grand Old Opry on Saturday night.

The Philco Cathedral, so called because of its domed shape, clutched an addiction to static and squeals. The radio, the source of weather, news, farm produce prices, and a variety of local and national shows, gave me my first understanding of entertainment outside my home town.

I recall local amateur musicians, snort and catch your breath preachers, and ads featuring a variety of cure-all tonics including Peptikon, Hatacol, Carter's Pills, and Black Draught. Each possessed a varying degree of "medicinal power."

National broadcasts programmed for children filled up the pre-supper hour from 5:00-6:00 p.m. Each evening, Monday thru Friday, two 30-minute dramas such as *Nick Carter Private Detective, The Shadow Knows, The Green Hornet*, and a parade of westerns including Bobby Benson and the B Bar B, the Lone Ranger, Hop-along-Cassidy, and everyone's favorites—Roy Rogers and Gene Autry. Earlier in the afternoon, housewives feasted on soap operas that to coin a phrase were really "clean and real-life events" sponsored by Duz, Oxidol, Old Dutch Cleanser, and Ivory Soap ("it floats").

Saturday night listeners in the south gave reverence to the Grand Old Opry live from the Ryman Auditorium in Nashville, Tennessee over clear channel WSM. I was too young to remember President Roosevelt's Fireside Chats and the announcement of the end of World War II. Nevertheless, I recall vividly my parents describing the importance of those events that came to them by radio.

Radio caught the attention of the listener's ear. Dramatic shows produced live required a wide variety of sound effects to duplicate horses running, car tires squealing, doors opening and closing, and a vast array of assorted other sounds. The radio effort's general intention focused on stimulating imagination to assist listeners to experience the vicarious roles in dramas, plays, and even situation comedies. Radio's power during the 30s, 40s and 50s magnified imagination and offered people snatches of time away from economic plight, the horror stories of war, and even the fear of the escalating nuclear threat. Sometimes work, as a daily routine, was adjusted to enjoy radio pleasures that lifted the soul out of hard times into the atmospheres of music, clean comedy, laughter, and even romance. I still recall the 6:30 Monday thru Friday national news commentators such as Gabriel Heater, Fulton J. Kathenborn, and Edward R. Murrow. These gentlemen held covenants of trust with listeners. Their previous day's report became next day's quotes. Radio grabbed hold of the mind, stirred the emotional juices, and produced an integrity spoken as, "I heard it on the radio."

My introduction to the movies began with Friday night trips to Forrest, Mississippi to the drive-in picture show. Once inside the darkened area in front of the screen, Dad parked the car, hung the speaker on the car window, and we waited for the show to begin. Usually we stopped by and picked up my Uncle Ed and his wife, Minnie Lee. One night during intermission between the feature show and the western, the Porch brothers sent me to the concession stand for popcorn and Cokes. The lady behind the canteen sensed my dismay as she handed five bags of popcorn and five cups of Coke to me. In care, she arranged the food in a flimsy Baby Ruth box top, and I began the long, tedious walk back to the car, determined not to slosh out the drinks or spill the buttered popcorn. I made it to the car. Next came the challenge to hand the whole lid of refreshments through the open window. I never understood why Aunt Minnie Lee did not open the door. As a rather portly and protrusive lady, maybe she merely refrained from extra movement. Anyway, as I lifted the food-packed lid through the window, the flimsy box folded in the middle and 60 ounces of Coke and ice and at least a peck of popcorn dumped into Aunt Minnie Lee's lap amidst her quick movement and panic, screams, and cries. Immediate effort to assist my sticky, ice-covered, soggy-popcorned Aunt Minnie Lee ended in a desperate trip back to her house, and I missed the western—a significant loss in my education.

Then one day, a rumor began running through town. The talk began at Holmes Barber Shop, moved down to the loafer's bench outside the post office, across to Wingate's Café, on through Margie's Beauty Parlor, and my Mamma delivered the news to Daddy at his blacksmith shop—a picture show was coming to town. Prior to the grand opening of our Park Theater, the fearful impact of the invasion of Hollywood into Pelahatchie resulted in sermons, a PTA called meeting that cancelled the assembly of the Mary Francis Chapter 222 of the Order of the Eastern Star, and a review of the town ordinances by the mayor and board of aldermen. But the show went on.

The Saturday afternoon 10¢ matinee usually included a Superman or Batman and Robin serial, Popeye, Bugs Bunny or Mickey Mouse cartoon, and maybe a sing-along clip with a bouncing ball. Comedians like Abbott and Costello, the Bowery Boys, and Little Rascals just made you laugh. Then life got real serious. Intermission meant, "Settle down; the western feature will soon begin."

The horse operas usually followed a fairly predictable plot. Someone greedy or devious did bad stuff on the ranch or in the community. In desperation, fearful of an invasion of masked crime, the good people would blame the local peace officer for ineffectiveness or inability to handle crime. Inevitably, a two-gun stranger (exception, Gene Autry only wore one gun) wearing a white hat rode into town, drank milk at the saloon, and eventually emerged to capture the villains following a horse chase scene while firing 50 shots from a six shooter without reloading. Once justice prevailed, he either rode off toward the west, sometimes only after telling the pretty girl he would return. Some later westerns did include a kiss. Yuck stuff when you're 10 years old. Our parents trusted the theater owner. They just expected the Saturday afternoon matinee to provide a good safe time for the kids. The owner honored the unwritten trust, knowing his respect for those parents could not be negotiated. He honored our local mores and apparently held no desire to expose kids of P town to a gross or ugly world.

Black and white television first arrived in metropolitan Pelahatchie when Mr. Pat, owner of the Western Auto, put up a 40-foot antenna in his yard to attract prospective TV customers. Many Saturday nights his wife Inez, as a marketing venture, invited folks over for the *Hit Parade* and *Gun Smoke* on Channel 12. Our family held an advantage due to Miss Inez being my Mamma's longtime friend. Soon the Ross brothers began selling Admiral TVs and "come to town on Saturday" folks gathered for the broadcast of the baseball game of the week on Saturday afternoon, another effective marketing venture. Between innings, fans would rush over to Goodman's Grocery Store or Rhode's Drug Store for cold drinks or ice cream. Throughout the early 1950s, a TV antenna beside a house or attached to a chimney signaled a new family status. At night, the bright screen could be seen through a window. If people desired added status, they left the TV box on the front porch for weeks after the purchase. Eventually another station, an NBC affiliate, offered another option. At that point, discussions began in our house directed toward buying a TV. Dad balked on the premise that TV was a passing fad. Mamma countered with her educational promotion. The tradeoff resulted in the decision for a cash buy out of money saved up over a year, funds normally spent going to the State Fair. Dad bucked the antenna thing as a point of principle. Therefore, our set drew signals through a rabbit ear apparatus. After months of snow and fuzz on the screen, he gave in for a $19 outside antenna.

I hold sweet memories of good time television. The programs included *Wide, Wide World, I Love Lucy, You Are There, Burns and Allen, Tennessee Ernie Ford, Gun Smoke, Have Gun Will Travel, Big Top*—shows all subject to interruption by messages from the President during this Cold War era. Then sadly one Sunday evening, a TV program changed our lives forever and fired the shot that killed Baptist Training Union—Elvis Presley appeared on *The Ed Sullivan Show*. Gradually, America at large entered the immerging "anything goes on" TV era that prevails today.

Aaron, as I channel surf outside your presence, a flood of memories come back to the good times that you have missed through the medium of more innocent television, radio, and Saturday afternoon movies. Those days a defined moral consciousness prevailed amidst the caution to honor the perspectives of the views of the public. In the event anything appeared risqué, the power of the on and off switch was exercised. You today are subject to much apparent as well as subliminal, provocative, and suggestive messages through the medium of television. The sensitivity of your wonder and imagination has been greatly diminished through television and movies over against the power of radio. I grieve for you. I grieve for the fact that what I received through those mediums was a blessing that you cannot enjoy today. Therefore, this epistle is dedicated to letting you in on a little bit of the entertainment style of my earlier day, lest you not at least have an opportunity to know there was a different time when the pure intention of entertainment won out over the power of economics, and the Barnum and Bailey principle to outdo the last show. Quite possibly as the pure novelty of the mediums of radio, movies and TV wore off, the addiction to sensationalism bowed to vulgarity, biased opinions, and unimaginative fantasy that sealed the tomb on the age of entertainment's innocence.

Passing on values with hope,

Paw Paw

One Lie, One High Price

Rehoboth Hill
Cane Ridge, TN

Dear Aaron,

March winds usually stir my memory of one of my naughty boy experiences.

This letter may move some readers from interest to intrigue, expecting sordid details. Paw Paw did something really bad. Actually, I hope my inadequate behavior at 10 years of age leaves a lesson that a bad choice may hurt you a long time later, even when you have forgotten your mistake.

Early March for me as a kid meant kite flying weather. The winds, if played right, could send a kite flying high and stopped only when I ran out of string.

My 10 year-old kite flying episode began at Mr. Cee's drugstore one March afternoon after school. The previous Saturday, I had earned a quarter turning the blower for Dad in his shop, all the time looking forward to Monday kite day.

A blue, red, or yellow kite composed of two balsa wood sticks, paper cover, and instructions for assembly and tying the kite bridle cost 15 cents. The purchase of a 200-foot ball of cotton string took my other dime. Sales tax had not been discovered in Mississippi in those days.

The procedure of preparation for launching the diamond shaped paper construction followed a specific sequential process. First, wind all the string off the pasteboard cylinder onto a stick 10-12 inches long, being careful not to tangle or wind the cotton twine too tightly. As the kite rose into the air, the string would roll off the stick easily. Second, cross the two sticks and hook each of the four ends into a stick notch at the four corners of the kite. Third, carefully punch a tiny hole near the top and bottom of the vertical stick and push the two ends of a short piece of string through each tear, tying the string ends to the wooden kite frame, thereby forming the bridle. <u>Fourth</u>, attach the long ball of string to the bridle. <u>Fifth</u>, add a tail made of small light pieces of cloth to provide better stability. Actually, we had two groups of kite flyers—tail flyers and non tail flyers. <u>Sixth</u>, lay the kite bridle side up and walk away about 10 steps. Now if the wind cooperated, you were prepared to do a series of test flights. <u>Finally</u>, gently pull the kite, hand held high over your head, as you begin running, slowly pick up speed. Usually after a few trips on a windy day, the kite would soar on up into the sky, pulling on the unwinding string provided you could avoid power lines and tree branches.

That fateful March Monday after buying my kite and string, I ran to the old football field near our house to join a few friends already successfully launching their paper and light wood kites.

Intentionally, carefully, I followed all—I mean *all*—the process. As I began running and hoping I was moving against the wind, my kite suddenly rose quickly about 15 feet into the air and immediately nose-dived even more rapidly, slamming into God's good and hard earth. Both sticks of the frame snapped and ripped long tears in the paper.

Despair, disappointment, and anger settled in all over me. For sure, my afternoon of aeronautical adventure had ended.

Now for the rest of the story. A kite when purchased came tightly rolled up, appearing to be in one piece. A maybe well-meaning friend, Billy Dan _____, came over, observed the disaster and suggested, "Why don't you roll the kite back up, go back up to the drugstore and tell old man Cee it was torn up when you unraveled it?" Now, I knew his solution was wrong. But folks, I had lost 15 cents. So armed with Billy Dan's solution, I ran back downtown, walked into the drugstore and showed Mr. Cee the "damaged kite" I had bought earlier that day. He carefully examined the mess of paper, string, and stick and replied looking straight at me, "You're sure this kite was like this when you unrolled it?" Meekly, weakly, I replied, "Yes, sir." He sighed, "Okay. I don't sell damaged goods. Do you want a new kite or 15 cents?" I took the new kite.

There's still more to this story. Six years later, Mr. Cee advertised in his drugstore window "Wanted—after school help for the soda fountain. Sixteen years of age or older." By then I knew Mr. Cee as deacon, church treasurer, church choir member, church Sunday school teacher. And I was James in everything at church for youth, Milton and Lillian's fine boy Porch. So I went in to apply for the job, making my case of needing to earn money for college. Confidently, I knew I would get the job. When I went by the drugstore the next day, he told me had hired Bill—one of my friends. Shocked, disappointed, I remember walking home wondering why I did not get the job. Sometime later and more mature, I came to the realization I really lost the soda fountain job all because of a 15-cent fib. I really believe he knew I fibbed about the kite six years earlier.

If indeed my conclusion is accurate, apparently I created a lack-of-trust issue that overshadowed my young life in a small town.

Aaron, along your way through life I hope you live each day with a consciousness you are indeed accountable for all of your actions.

Passing on values with hope,

Paw Paw

Flag's Up, School's In

Rehoboth Hill
Cane Ridge, TN

Dear Aaron,

My best memories of grades eight thru twelve began at the school flag pole. The tall structure, welded sections of galvanized pipe with a ball and windless apparatus on top, had been constructed during the days of the Great Depression.

In our school, grades one thru seven attended classes on the back side of the building and thus had limited access to the flag pole.

Beginning with the 8th grade, students rose to the dignity of front door access to school. Each day pupils encountered the pole, even if only to walk around the tall edifice.

Minutes before 8:00 a.m. my first day in the 8th grade, our school principal, Mr. J. O. Rutledge, handed me a folded American flag and instructed, "James, raise the flag so I can ring the morning bell." I ran out to the pole having no idea how to raise that flag. The small link chain with two tennis shoe strings attached about 30 inches apart hung limply from the pole. Quickly, I tied the flag to the chain using the shoestrings. That's all I knew to do. As I was pulling the chain, surprisingly the flag climbed the pole. Throughout the day, I looked out classroom windows to make sure Old Glory fluttered in the autumn breeze.

Later in the day, Mr. J.O. informed me my responsibility included lowering and folding the flag at the close of the school day. Lowering—no problem. Folding—big challenge. Actually, only the help of my Boy Scout handbook enabled me to conquer the folding job. The following morning, our principal spied me out for the same assignment. On that morning, I got his message! He expected me to attend to that flag continuously. In those days, the rules of American flag decorum were very specific and respectful. The flag never flew during rain. The American flag never touched the ground. My task included honoring those national traditions. My last day of high school, five years later, I raised, lowered, and folded that same American flag for the last time. The following fall, school for the town's kids and teenagers began in a different location with new facilities. Today I occasionally wonder whatever happened to that Old Glory.

From time to time during the five-year flag interval, my father expressed a sense of appreciation to me for my respect of the flag duty. Evidently once he concluded I would see my responsibility through, he told me his story of growing respect to honor Old Glory and his country.

Late one afternoon in June 1918 before boarding a train the next day for Camp Shelby, Mississippi, my doughboy father locked his blacksmith shop, walked to the house his parents shared with him, slept well, and early that morning the Rankin County draftee went off to World War I because "it was the right thing to do." Later in life, he shared his reluctance to travel. According to Buck Private Porch, he had seen all the world he wanted to see at the United States Government's expense during World War I.

Following very "basic" training in hot, humid south Mississippi and persevering thru another long train trip, this time to New York City, my Dad-to-be and his company boarded an old leaky troop ship and wallowed across the north Atlantic, constantly in fear of German submarines. Landing in Brest, France, the 139th Field Artillery unloaded their equipment, marched inland, and then rode slow moving trucks to a staging area.

On his first day as a visitor to France, he began the routine of drilling and training followed by weeks of waiting to go up to the front. His recounting of the experience focused on his remembrance of cold, rain, bad food, home sickness, and constant griping by comrades existing in harsh unsanitary conditions. The camp rumor focused on the next major push by the AEF on through France and into the Argonne Forest. By the way, AEF stood for American Expeditionary Forces. To the American soldier, AEF meant "after England fails." Dad's actual battle time was averted by the November 11, 1918 Armistice. Somehow, his unit received immediate orders to return to the states and by early December boarded the U.S.S. George Washington to sail for the good ol' USA. Days later, just prior to entering New York Harbor, private Porch's name appeared on the duty roster to patrol the deck as the ship neared the Statue of Liberty. Officers feared men would rush to the rail on the starboard side of the ship. The weight of the quick movement of the troops could affect the balance and direction of the ship and safety of the soldiers. Dad confessed that once Miss Liberty came into view, he neglected his orders. "I was so glad to see that sign of America I went to the rail myself." Over 80 years later flying out of New York to Portugal one night, I saw that same Miss Liberty and remembered the 30-year-old soldier on his homeward trip.

Still hoping to be home for Christmas, the troops reported to Camp Merrits, New Jersey. Following a long, long trip over and back, weary and yet unwounded or disabled, he and many of his comrades contracted—of all things—mumps. The entire camp, quarantined by the virus, spent Christmas Day in the camp hospital with little merriment. Dad filled in a painful detail. The Army Mess Sergeant served each of the mumps boys a big grapefruit for Yuletide lunch.

Finally in January after his honorable discharge, Private J.M. Porch, Sr. of Company D of the 139th Field Artillery stepped on the Illinois Central east bound train late one afternoon in Jackson, Mississippi in route to good old Pelahatchie, Mississippi, twenty five miles away in the final ride home.

At this point in the often told story, I would ask, "What did you do then?" Contact with his parents had been limited to two postcards. "Son, I walked straight home from the depot to see about my Mamma and Daddy. The next morning, I walked downtown and opened up my shop, ready to work."

Dad went to war in response to duty, served out his tour of service, and came home. I never sensed a matter of fact perception from him. Rather, I heard him say in his genuine attitude, "My war service was the right thing to do."

On Monday morning, May 9, 1960, I sat beside my mother under a funeral home tent. Immediately in front of us, only inches away, a flag-covered bronze casket lay nestled over a grave dug deep in the red Mississippi clay. At the appropriate time following a 21 gun salute and *Taps*, two Mississippi National Guardsmen stepped forward, removed the flag from the casket, folded it with military precision, and placed Old Glory gently in my Mother's hands. The guardsmen spoke with compassion. I only remember one phrase, "From a grateful Nation." That flag, never unfurled and resting now in a walnut case, occupies an often looked upon place in our home today. One day I'll hand it on to you with my treasure of memories from a patriot soldier who did his best duty to his country and never disrespected the flag.

Reflecting back, I know his story of his American idea became known to me only after he knew I would carry on his honor for the Stars and Stripes.

Aaron, you—the next generation, are now learning of your past. Yes, this past is part of you, and you hold the responsibility as an American citizen living in our God-blessed nation to keep the trust with the symbol of our country all the years God gives you ahead.

Passing on values with hope,

Paw Paw

Bible Memorization by Painful Motivation

Rehobth Hill
Cane Ridge, TN

Dear Aaron,

Being promoted to the Junior Department in the Pelahatchie Baptist Church Sunday School constituted a right of passage for a Junior boy.

Mr. Knox Ross, already a legend to each of us, taught the class. A World War II marine and veteran of the Battle of Iwo Jima, he operated a cattle farm, worked for state government, and alternated between Beechnut chewing tobacco and smoking Roi-Tan Cigars. A man's man in our eyes. As younger boys we heard stories about Knox's Sunday school class. We knew the extracurricular activities included watermelon cuttings, wiener roasts, peanut boilings, ice cream freezes, and possibly other Mr. Knox's surprises.

What we failed to understand was that each Sunday morning during Sunday school class, each person was expected to stand and quote the memory verse by heart. In the event that a young man did not have his verse memorized, Knox would usher him down to his mother's class, usually the Timothy, Eunice, Lois Class, and pronounce the ultimate embarrassment— "These boys did not know the memory verse in my class today. I believe you mamas needed to know so they can be better prepared next Sunday." Then you had to stand in front of your mother's class and recite the special verse, hastily memorized during the previous 30 minutes. Actually, for most of us only one long journey down to the first floor of the church proved to be a sufficient learning experience. I can remember also that those who did not know their verse could be taunted by their peers such as, "You didn't know your verse in Knox's class this morning." The word would spread out across the church. During the coming week at school, you could be reminded you did not know your Bible verse on

57

Sunday. There were even occasions when it was the topic of conversation in Holmes' Barber Shop.

So, consistently along about 7:00 p.m. each Saturday night, I would hear my mother's familiar question, "Have you learned your memory verse for tomorrow?" I would open my Junior Sunday School quarterly, praying that the great writers from the Baptist Sunday School Board in the faraway Baptist haven of Nashville, Tennessee had selected a very short verse. I only remember one occasion when the verse was "Jesus wept." The words of Jesus were considered to be the easier verses to memorize. Somehow, Paul's writings became entangled in our minds and offered much more of a challenge. However, whatever the verse, we knew that on Sunday morning in the upstairs Junior Department Mr. Ross would be waiting for our recitation.

I look back on those occasions now with intensely much more appreciation than in the early 1950s. Through the Bible reading provided by my mother and the expectation of a fine Christian deacon named Knox, I gained a better understanding of the value of the Word of God, and many of the verses that I committed to memory just to keep from going to my mama's sunday school class are now indelibly fixed in my mind. "Thy Word have I hid in my heart." What a value!

Passing on values with hope,

Paw Paw

Just Equal Folks All Around Town

Rehoboth Hill
Cane Ridge, TN

Dear Aaron,

Yes, the Bible tells us that God created people on the sixth day, just before He rested. God affirmed His own creation by declaring His work was "very good."

Sadly, very sadly, before too long you will discover, how do I say this— some not so nice people. The non-nice come in all sizes, shapes, colors, and both sexes. No group claims any isolation. Sometimes, these humans become a pure nuisance and magnify their obsession with self-importance. You may wonder, "Where did these people come from?" since God made very good folk and He cares for all people. A word of caution —don't try to figure them out. Rather, learn to live among them and love them. Some will never change. Besides, God can handle them.

During my growing up years, our town had its share of the "un-nice." One I especially remember was known as the community smart-aleck. *Webster's Dictionary* cannot help you with the definition. In fact, I do not know whether the word is spelled "eleck" or "aleck." Big deal! Basically, an "intellectual-aleck" is short on wisdom and long on pride in what he thinks he knows that everyone else should know about. He or she allows what they think they know get in the way of what they really know. Basically, these people work hard on being arrogant. One of these (our area had several) took a trip up North and returned to tell everyone about his tour of Mayonnaise mines.

My primary subject for this letter I simply call "J.W." A gentleman farmer, a local celebrated smart-aleck, he never got dirty giving orders to "his hands." He drove a clean white pickup bearing no residual of farm life. (Explanation available upon request.)

One *very* hot late June afternoon, my blacksmith father was laboring intensely to sharpen some plow points to enable two African American farmers to get back to their field as soon as possible. Knee-high corn needed dirting, and the middles run out. The farmers rested patiently in the shop talking with Dad and awaiting the completion of his work. The atmosphere in Mr. Milton's blacksmith shop in mid-summer Mississippi resulted from a combination of sun heat on a tin roof and thermal energy from a cloud of coal smoke plus the glare of flames in the forge. But things were about to get hotter through the arrogance of the certain un-nice fellow and my Dad's dramatic emotion. As a 10 year-old boy, resting his Dad by turning the air blower to the forge and attentively listening to his "Speed up" or "Slow down" directions to maintain the proper heat in the fire pan, I was about to observe a lifelong, lasting lesson.

Suddenly, we heard the sound of a fast approaching truck. J.W. drove furiously in the lineage of Jehu down the dirt road in front of the shop and slammed on the brakes, stopping near the front door. His hurry filled the steaming shop with dust. He jumped out of his farm chariot, reached into the bed of the pickup, retrieved an object and ran into the shop disregarding and ignoring the two African American farmers patiently waiting for Dad to sharpen their plows. He laid a broken Pittman rod on the anvil and announced, "Porch fix this right now; I've got to get back to the hay field." (OK, it's agricultural emergency definition time.) A Pittman Rod, a strong section of hickory or hard oak about 3 ½ feet long, has brass couplings on each end and is designed to carry power from the turning wheel of a mower or tractor to the sickle blade. A broken Pittman rod, and no hay gets cut.

My father leisurely reached over to the anvil and picked up the broken rod, examined it in the presence of the two African American farmers, and while he made his diagnosis I wondered, "Mr. J.W. said, 'Fix this right now,' and there are two men here that have been waiting for Dad to finish their work. What was my father going to do?"

Still, never speaking, Dad, carrying the Pittman rod in his hand, walked to the front of the shop. Across the road, kudzu vines and blackberry vines covered a vacant lot. Still silent, Dad with J.W.'s Pittman rod in his right hand, reared back and threw the mower part as far as he could over into the tangled undergrowth. Then he turned and spoke, "J.W., if you want that thing fixed, go find it and get in line." In my father's place of business, regardless of who you were, you waited your turn.

I don't recall that the event had any long-term effect on Mr. J.W. He did find the Pittman rod, left it to be fixed, and returned the next week. As to the African American farmers, possibly in a day in which they were unwelcome in white churches, watched movies from the balcony of the town theater, were denied restroom privileges, and even stepped off the sidewalk as white ladies passed, they had an equal and respected place in my Daddy's blacksmith shop.

Aaron, the Bible verse accompanying this letter goes as follows: "And God created man in his own image, in the image of God He created him; male and female he created them." (Genesis 1: 27) As I write this letter, I'm searching diligently around in these verses to find whether there were any exceptions. Since I have found none, and even with my limited Biblical understanding, I believe that God included *all* people as equals and made no exceptions. As to a succinct commentary on the verse, "God did not make any junk."

Passing on values with hope,

Paw Paw

By God's Grace, a Table Prepared

Rehoboth Hill
Cane Ridge, TN

Dear Aaron,

Growing up, we, Miss Lillian, Big Milton, and I ate well!

Actually, we ate well only by the bounty of the grace of the Father and my folks' hard work.

Extending out in three directions from our house, our fertile garden patches grew vegetables from late February to the end of October. Irish potatoes sprouting by the end of February gave my Daddy a sign of the smile of God. I remember pulling fresh turnip greens on Halloween day. During that annual eight-month interval, we focused all available time, sweat, and energy on plowing and planting, plowing and hoeing, plowing and fertilizing, plowing and watering, plowing again, and waiting. We held tenaciously to our hope for sunshine and rain, and feared wind storms and hail. The crops included Kentucky Wonder snap beans, Purple-Hulled peas, Gulf State and Marigold tomatoes, Trucker's Favorite corn, Green yams, Nancy Hall, and Puerto Rican sweet potatoes, Cow Horn okra, yellow Crooked-neck squash, Bermuda onions, cucumbers (yuk), Black-diamond watermelons, red-topped beets, gray pumpkins, lettuce, peanuts, and bell pepper. The effort defied any idea of a hobby. Rather, those prayed-over patches and their bounty were intended to provide fresh vegetables through the summer and feed the family throughout the coming fall and winter.

I hold precious vivid memories shadowing my Dad or catching his big rough work hand as we almost daily inspected the garden fields. He taught me to hoe, hill-drop seed, knock off the tops of rows, clean out middles, carefully side dress plants with fertilizer, set out tomato plants with ample water, lay Nancy Hall sweet potato slips in an open row and gently pull the dirt over them. He showed me the way to gently squeeze an ear of corn to determine its maturity. On my knees in early spring, I scratched under new potato vines to pull out a few spuds for boiling and then gently closed the hole with dirt. My "expertise" leaned much more toward hand tools—rakes, hoes, shovels, and forks. A mule and I seldom ever really got it together. Apparently, my eye sight limited my plowing to crooked and uneven rows. More honestly, my aversion to the view ahead when plowing retarded my adjustment to the process. Maybe my best memory settled in late one summer as I got the knack of thumping a ripe watermelon. Oh, the joy when what's thumped and heard to be ripe turned out red when a sharp knife sliced through the melon.

This narrative could go on and on into boredom. I have a point. My entire participation, not only by choice but by parental expectation and eventually my gradual realization, helped me connect what I ate with the good Father's created fertile dirt. Working in the earth, feeling the soil dribble through my hands or as mud squeezes through my fingers, and breathing in the aroma of fresh-broken sod linked me forever to the source of my life-sustaining food. Even as a child, I seemed to participate in a covenant with the Creator, a covenant even today beyond my understanding of His surprising grace.

Once gathering time arrived, we picked, dug, pulled, and gathered whatever God grew with our work and carried the precious bounty to Mom in the kitchen. My understanding of the power of uniqueness and creativity began with Mom's cooking. Vegetables can be plain, insipid, and dull. Oh, not in Miss Lillian's hands. Field corn simmering in real butter in a black skillet with a delicate balance of salt and pepper came to the table to bypass your teeth and garnish your taste buds. Fried okra had to cook slow, be dipped out at the exact point of crispness, and drained well. Peas required a large piece of serrated salt sow belly with the rind remaining on to pull out the ultimate pea taste to flavor pot liquor. My Mother's culinary efforts all focused on a process of preparing raw food items for family nourishment with major emphasis on taste. As I remember, all her cooking involved proper heat, delicate mixture of ingredients, elapsed time, and sensitivity. Heat came from a wood and later a gas stove. Both wood and gas stoves require an innate ability to regulate the proper heat. Prepared food usually required some mixing, extending from basic salt and pepper to more intricate recipes demanding mixtures at specific times in the process. Mom took great pride in owning an electric mixer. The day the appliance died, Dad undertook to provide maintenance. His repeated "fix-it" efforts resulted in various mixtures of leftover parts. So spoons and spatulas replaced the old mixer. Time mainly meant how much, how little, how long, how short a cooking period. As to sensitivity, Mom knew the meaning of bubbles, rolling boils, aromas of cooking foods at precise moments in the preparation and changes in smells as the mixture of ingredients changed. Finally, only as an experienced southern culinary expert she knew when to declare, "It's done." Pie with piled-high meringue only could be removed from the stove when the drops of "sweet sweat" appeared both in the valleys and hills of the egg whites. Fried chicken, pot roast, and fried pork chops required heavy cooking vessels, mainly black iron skillets and thick aluminum pots. Proper heat inside such containers produced chemical reactions beyond explanation, even to taste buds. My Mamma, one of nine sisters, all claimed specialty dishes. Aunt Lucille majored on hard brown crust thin cornbread. Miss Lillian's skillet cornbread began as home grown corn ground into meal at Grover Wadsworth's mill. Mamma made thick bread for a purpose. She refried leftover bread soaked in butter as a compliment to suppertime leftovers. Oh, the joy of good and bad cholesterol.

Many of our serving dishes bore the imprint "U.S. Navy." Soon after World War II, my folks bought bowls, plates, saucers and cups, and metal ware shipped back from the South Pacific. These items, priced at five and ten cents, could be acquired simply by shopping at an Army-Navy surplus store.

Our meals, almost without exception, appeared three times a day hot, fresh, and appetizing in smell and appearance. Once set, all the family sat at the same table and awaited Dad's blessing. His simple, brief prayer of gratitude called us to a halt with bowed heads, closed eyes, and a settling quietness. Once again our brief worship connected us to the Heavenly Father, the Provider of the bounty on the table.

So pass the field peas, fried corn, sliced tomatoes, hot cornbread, and gravy-laden country fried steak, and fill up my glass with 40-weight sweet tea and give me elbow room. Only my Heavenly Father can set such a table with such food grace.

Passing on values with hope,

Paw Paw

Revenge Really Hurts

Rehoboth Hill
Cane Ridge, TN

Dear Aaron,

My mother, your great "Sweet Mom," seldom missed a chance to teach me a big lesson, even if her curriculum required inflicting extreme and painful measures.

I vividly recall the afternoon my naughtiness set her off on a teachable moment about conscience. An urge, inner voice, unique feeling—all have been used to identify the indefinable human conscience. My best shot in describing conscience is recognizing I have the chance to do right over against wrong while still leaning toward the right act. Possibly the inadequacy of those words can be helped through a story. As you know, Paw Paw's disdain for definition makes room for his stories. The following event, verified in the chronicles of Pelahatchie, abused my young illustrious reputation, but I survived.

Mr. John Cauthen, a late octogenarian in my home town, leisurely strolled past my boyhood home four times each day, six days a week (on Sunday he made one trip to the Methodist church). Daily, only prevented by extreme inclement weather, he made his town walk dressed in a seasonal suit, hat, white shirt and tie, brightly shined shoes, and carrying a walking stick. In the 1940's, he held the distinction as a "dandy." A retired single fellow (though nobody knew his earlier vocation), he appeared even to a six year old as a dressed up, very serious old fellow who cared little for children.

Our family home sat beside a gravel road apart from other houses, so much of my outside playtime included the constant companionship of my little dog, Bobo.

One hot July noontime, Mr. John came down the road going home to mid-day dinner (he lived with his sister). As he passed the front porch of our house, Bobo, who never knew a stranger, ran out, tail wagging to greet Bro. Cauthen. Immediately, the elderly gentleman hit Bobo on the head and across the back with his walking stick and uttered quickly, harshly some words I had never heard before. Bobo cowered down, cried and squealed and ran back to me shaking and whimpering. I picked up my little abused dog and ran into the house. Mama came to my rescue, offering comfort to both her son and his devoted friend. She knew my hurt and anger, and lovingly and patiently rationalized, "Everyone does not like dogs. Maybe Bobo scared Mr. John. Possibly our elderly friend has been attacked at some time earlier by a dog. He did not mean to hurt Bobo." Her final counsel must have really pushed my button, "James, it is over. Let's tell God we forgive Mr. John and then you go back and play."

Mama's wise parental rationale did not work. While I could not label my intentions or all of my feelings, I was already bent on revenge. Putting Bobo in his back yard pen, I watched for Mr. John to return to town after "dinner." As he slowly climbed the hill leading to our house, I went outside and began to uncoil 50 feet of water hose attached to the yard faucet. (Some of these details were related to me years later by my Mother.) According to Mama, I began watering her flower beds with the hose nozzle on full force. Once the dog abuser reached a spot just in front of our house, I ran out and wet that old man from head to toe. Once again I heard new words, this time in a very high pitched voice. Mama, alerted by Mr. John's cussing, ran out this time to rescue my enemy. She picked up his hat, retrieved his walking stick, helped him to a chair on the front porch, and brought out towels to dry off the old fellow, all the time apologizing for my behavior amidst Mr. John's silence. Once Mr. John calmed down and dried out a bit, Mama carried the dog-beater home after giving me a stern command to sit still on the porch "until I come back." I knew I was in big trouble.

After driving back into the driveway, Mama hastily walked up onto the front porch, pointed to a nearby peach tree and commanded, "Go get me a long switch." My fear jumped a notch as I remembered I was wearing short pants. I got a whooping that left welts on my legs for days. Child abuse? Oh, no! Child discipline? Yes! Then Mama began the dreaded talk with a question, "Did you feel better after you wet Mr. John?" Honestly, at that moment all I felt was the stinging, burning, welts on my precious little legs. She continued, "James, you decided to hurt Mr. John because he hurt Bobo, didn't you?" Painfully, I answered, "Yes ma'am." Then she made her big point, "Son, you never feel better hurting someone because they hurt you."

Years later, I learned the label for that episode—revenge, and understood Mama's counsel. Revenge is never sweet, or in the words of our Living Lord Jesus Christ, "Vengeance is mine, I will repay."

Now a final confession, I cannot plead consistency in practicing the old teaching or claim innocence from temptations to get back at someone who brings hurt on my life or family. However, by His grace, I keep trying to let go and abide by my Savior's expectation.

Passing on values with hope,

Paw Paw

RANGING, Expanding Trust

Rehoboth Hill
Cane Ridge, TN

Dear Aaron,

Ready or not, I'm sending you a new word—<u>Ranging</u>. The term, as I remember, never made the dictionary. Besides, you already know Paw Paw's aversion to the dictionary. The word book becomes a crutch. No word meaning can be conveyed in any one statement. I prefer attempts to understand a word.

The sermonette is over! Now for my explanation of ranging—"my gradual process as a child moving freely away from the home place while honoring Mama and Daddy's limits and respecting their trust while being acutely aware of the consequences."

Such a venture for me began the Christmas Santa Claus brought me wheels—a bicycle.

Breakpoint!

Why now this letter? Simply, I ranged in a time when a child alone on a bicycle rode without fear. Oh, Aaron, how I wish you could grow up in a safer world. I hold both pain and anger together that we parents and grandparents bear the stress of watch out and watch over for weirdoes, freaks, and perverts in today's crazy world. Besides, you will probably never live in a time where folks naturally looked out for and watched over other folk's kids, slept behind unlocked doors, and knew trust, not as a presumption but as a gift. Once again, once upon my growing up time, a child alone was safe out in this local world.

Okay, back to my wheels. The Christmas morning surprise, interrupted by a trip to Grandmama's, meant delay to my bicycle riding lessons. Dad limited his help to basic start up and stop, getting on and getting off. I recall his words I would soon understand, "I can't teach you to balance yourself." And so, the learning by riding began. First time, on and away and down I went with a fear of falling and fear of damage to the precious bicycle. Through the following weeks, I mastered my technique, even starting off on my left foot and throwing my right leg over the seat like the bigger boys. Originally, Milton and Lillian limited my riding area to around the house and as far as the Methodist church and back—all within sight of the house. That routine soon lost the sense of adventure. Following weeks of persistent begging, Mama agreed for me to ride all the way downtown to Dad's blacksmith shop. She scheduled the big venture for a certain Monday afternoon after school. Before leaving the house, she specifically outlined my route, all on streets or alleys with little traffic. I remember wondering about the carefully designed route including down Church Street, onto Broad Street, turn left and ride behind the Chevrolet place, turn left onto the sidewalk bordering Highway 80, and left again onto Ellis Alley—the narrow dirt trail leading to Dad's shop. I rode as told. The excitement displaced the strict designated route. Until! Turning onto Ellis Alley and seeing Daddy's shop straight ahead, I quickly understood the route plan. Mama, in accentuated parallel fashion, had driven a different route and arrived first. Her idea of a surprise wounded my young ego. I immediately concluded she had not trusted me, and I told her so. Dad responded, "Lillian, I asked you not to!" I began to get the message. My parents definitely would travel unparalleled tracks on extending me trust. Oh well, today they see this story from a Heavenly perspective. So, no big deal.

Gradually, my folk expanded the range limits. Eventually, I could ride the town. My last remembered set boundaries extended south to the creek bridge, north to Aunt Bessie's on State Highway 43, west to Aunt Lucille's on US Highway 80, and East all the way to Lucille Shiver's store. Each specific set-by-Mama point included for me a hint of suspicion. Aunt Bessie, Aunt Lucille, and Mrs. Shiver's, all members of the TEL Sunday School Class at the Baptist Church (and all parents), assuredly reported my travels each Sunday morning. I waited years to understand the creek bridge limit. Finally, I remembered—Betty Coats could see the creek bridge from her house. Bi-weekly she and Mama gathered as sainted sisters of the Mary Frances Chapter Number 222 of the Order of the Eastern Star. So, footnote now, after a half century I finally figured out the southern limit. I respected those limits, well almost, nearly, close to. Actually, this give and take ranging process worked well for me. They gradually gave me new area and I had the choice to take responsibility and in so doing earn their trust.

My ranging-trust side of childhood included a business responsibility. Dad's blacksmith shop customers included some who received weekly or monthly bills prepared by Mama. Once I learned to do readin', writin', and 'rithmetic he let me "fix" and deliver his bills by bicycle with the instructions, "Wait for the check or cash." To accommodate my "work bike," he bolted a Grapette drink case to my double header above the rear wheel fender. Later, we upgraded to a large wire basket adequate in size to hold two one gallon glass jars of fresh milk gently ridden home immediately after Mrs. Winsted milked and strained the fresh unpasteurized, nonhomogenized, no vitamin D added health food.

In all honesty, this bicycle ranging had less than the best moments. The Illinois Central trains passed through town several times a day. We dumb boys invented a risky, daring, dangerous game. "Let's beat the train across the depot crossing." Hesitantly, I'll describe that gamble game. When the train passes the John G crossing, ride fast from the ice house up the road paralleling the track, and ride across the depot crossing before the train passes. Short game! Mr. Billy "Shorty" Gaston, depot agent, Baptist deacon, choir bass, turned us in to our parents. Immediately, walking replaced bike riding for a season. Now the thought of those stupid stunts sends cold chills up my back.

A ranging bike could be a big problem. Failure to oil the chain heightened the risk of a broken link and walking the two-wheeler home. Riding up and down the Baptist church concrete steps raised the possibility of a flat tire. Worst of all, and most embarrassing, was the malady of hanging up your right britches leg between the chain and the peddle sprocket. Talk about total immobilization! You couldn't, yeah that too. So, cut it out with a pocket knife? (Each boy had a Barlow or Case two-blade.) No way! Got to get home for help. Time for coast mode and one-foot push.

I rode alone or with a pack of friends countless miles around and through that good town. No major accidents. Nobody ever frightened us. Literally, we knew no reason to be afraid. Assuredly, the protective hand of the Living God of Grace took up a near position to and over us.

Aaron, such a time as my childhood under a wide umbrella of security will not return. No era ever returns. So on behalf of your family, we will diligently watch over you knowing Jesus watches even more, and better.

Passing on values with hope,

Paw Paw

P.S. The last time I saw the last part of that old bicycle, Dad had upgraded his metal wheel push plow with my bike's front wheel, enabling him to plow faster and easier through the corn rows in the garden.

Delicacies, Never Assumed

Rehoboth Hill
Cane Ridge, TN

Dear Aaron,

My summer time officially arrived when the day time temperature hit a Mississippi muggy 70 degrees or more. Such conditions signaled the coming of a variety of southern summer delicacies, special eating treats, all best prepared and eaten during the hot months of June, July and August, each one defying weight loss while raising cholesterol and blood sugar.

"Art is in the eye of the beholder." If so, a southern eating delicacy is in the mouth, across the teeth and gums, and down to the tummy. Each anatomical portion of the digestive system celebrates the good taste and nourishment. My priority belongs to scratch banana pudding. Such a concoction holds an aversion to boxed custard mix or Cool Whip topping. The traditional recipe for scratch banana pudding originally appeared on the Nabisco Vanilla Wafers box. No substitute would be honored. In recent years, because of cultural shifts, the makers of the cookie have chosen to substitute other seasonal recipes, replacing the standard for banana pudding. There is no other way to confess this sin against the future southern cooks. I wonder who will truly fall victim to perpetrating this affliction on banana pudding out of ignorance of the recipe. I am talking specifically about the stuff put in the pudding in addition to bananas and vanilla wafers. The actual pudding essence is indemnified through a mixture of eggs, milk, sugar, flour, and rapid steady progressive stirring in a pot immersed in a large vessel of hot water over an eye on top of a stove. The true texture and consistency for appropriate southern banana pudding cannot be prepared if this step is omitted. The great southern cooks spread the green tinged banana slices all over the bottom of a container then added a layer of Nabisco Wafers and more bananas, and finally, a generous topping of homemade pudding. The next step separated the cooks from ordinary to extraordinary. This came in the preparation of the meringue that would top the pudding. The egg white meringue beaten well and piled high will survive a few minutes in the oven for browning and produce ample drops of sweet sweat all over the delicious desert.

Truly, scratch banana pudding now is not a seasonal desert as in my childhood days. I vividly remember during the summer time when announcement would spread across town that Goodman's Grocery Store had a fresh stalk of bananas. Some would laugh at this fact; however, in the environment of my early years such an arrival of fresh tropical food in our town was an occasion for excitement.

Almost everybody raised tomatoes. Church talk, street talk, post office talk, and loafer bench talk during the month of June usually extended to the point, "How are your tomatoes doing?" The arrival of the first red ripe tomatoes meant the beginning of the tomato sandwich season. This is serious stuff. An improper manufactured tomato sandwich is not worth putting in hog slop. Therefore, I shall describe the proper procedure for the development of the southern delicacy, a tomato sandwich. Initially, select fresh store bought bread. Next apply real mayonnaise! None of that Miracle Whip junk. Off brand salad dressing should never grace a tomato sandwich. Real mayonnaise contains Wesson oil and hen eggs. You hold a slice of bread in the extended palm of your hand. Next, spread a copious amount of mayonnaise or mynaise. The nerd term "Mayo" had never even been invented or thought of during my childhood. Real mayonnaise must be thick enough to lump up on the bread and not fall off a spreading knife. Proceed then to peel and cut thick slices of red, juicy tomatoes large enough to cover the bread with plenty of lap over. The top stem slice with the hard white center never graces a sandwich. To use such a slice would constitute an abomination of desolation. Some folk prefer their tomato sandwiches with the peeling left on. Whatever! Salt and pepper the tomatoes and cover the exposed salted and peppered tomato with the remaining slice of bread. Leave the crust on! Crust trimmers reveal an aversion to their upbringing. Allow the delicacy to age for at least 15 minutes. Some of us, "good ole boys" on right occasions will be led to add bologna or liver cheese (goose liver). Eat with your mouth closed to savor the taste, and also to prevent air pressure from pushing mayonnaise slick tomatoes down your throat in chunks excessive to proper swallowing. Chew slowly, savoring each bite. Please remember a tomato sandwich is a seasonal delicacy denied from October through May. No southern boy or girl in their right mind would concoct a tomato sandwich using store bought, hot house tomatoes. And honestly, only on rare occasions can one tomato sandwich be adequate for a meal.

The appearance in our home of an ice cream freezer meant the coming of a special occasion. Only a few of the elect in a small southern community owned a Cold Mountain wood tub ice cream freezer. The item when not in use received careful protection from dust, salt corrosion, or rot to the wooden container. No appliance held the reputation of being worthy of being borrowed more than a hand turned freezer. Our family never owned one, but we knew who did and maintained close friendship with those folks. A wide variety of recipes for homemade vanilla ice cream evolved over the years. Recipes provided the topic for discussion during Sunday school class meetings, Eastern Star gatherings, family reunions, and especially Baptist ice cream suppers. I never knew if ice cream recipe made the agenda during the monthly bridge club meetings. Baptists in my town considered the bridge club folk as uppity, and all of them went to the Methodist church. Whatever the proportion mixture, southern homemade ice cream contained eggs, cream rising (nonhomogenized) milk, sugar, and vanilla extract. Proper care in the amount of the vanilla used in the recipe would determine the frozen consistency of the dessert. Vanilla extract contains alcohol, and too much of the flavoring would result in vanilla milkshake antifreeze. The genius of making homemade ice cream really depended on the right combination of ice and salt. At this delicate point in the process, many freezers of cream suffered from ignorance and/or inattention to details. Standard procedure for the best ice cream demanded alternate layers of ice and salt from bottom to top of freezer. Once frozen, the dasher had to be removed. There is nothing absolutely more exciting than for a child to stand watching the dasher being pulled out of an ice cream can knowing that ice cream hanging on the blades would be his or hers to enjoy. That's real living!

Aaron, space will only allow me to comment on one additional essential southern delicacy—southern 40-weight sweet tea. Simply stated, loose ground up tea leaves are added to boiling water and sugar. The concoction has to simmer for a time. Once cool and strained into a glass jug, the tea should be deep red in color. A batch of light red or amber color tea should be poured out. The process began again. Most southern ladies knew that the recipe on the Tetley or Lipton tea box should be doubled as to the amount of tea used in the process. I can well remember the appearance of 40-weight ice tea at revival meetings and dinner on the ground during rural church meetings. Usually someone in the neighborhood would buy a new galvanized wash tub and put a 50-pound block of ice in the tub. Then the tea would be poured over the ice, and everyone had the privilege to dip from the tub during lunch. Only on extreme rare occasions would lemon or lemon slices be available.

Aaron, once again thanks for traveling back with me through my descriptive memory and points of nostalgia. As I have indicated before, once upon a time in my childhood years, things were a lot different than they are today. My prayer is that your recognition of those times will be a part of your legacy even as a child of God.

These remembrances do not celebrate merely my nostalgia. Rather, the anecdotal approach to remembering life as it was a long time ago is really part of my God-given heritage. Our Heavenly Father intends that the seasons of life be connected and further expects us to learn from the previous to bless the present. I commend to you then my belief that even in matters that may sound trivial, such as delicacies of eating, there is the presence of God in caring for His people.

Passing on values with hope,

Paw Paw

Moving Along Learning Together

Rehoboth Hill
Cane Ridge, TN

Dear Aaron,

You attend school in the great information age. Today's computer technology enables you even in the elementary grades to sit in one place, touch a series of keys, and explore the world in sight and sound. While I harbor no jealousy, my elementary school era did require much more personal effort in the learning process. I label my way of learning more as discovery and adventure. Literally, I learned by going to the books. In the laptop epoch, data lies awaiting your touch of the keys.

The following descriptive windows into my grammar school days raise up fond memories and clue you in to school at a much slower pace mixed up with just being a child.

My first grade teacher, Miss Olla, was a stern lady who had missed all courses on humor and majored entirely on *her* way as the *only* way. We sat at tables, 10 aggressive scholars each in a low-to-the-floor chair, easily tipped over with minimal effort. By the end of the first day, all of the class mastered the art of the clunk sound, and notes went home outlawing chair flipping. One student, Billy Dan, didn't get the message and Miss Olla took him to the principal's office. Mr. N was a tall, long-toothed man who, according to upperclassmen, used his secret red electric paddle to administer punishment. Stories of bloodied, deformed students returning from his office sent terror through our class. We kids at the Baptist table prayed for the safe return of brother Billy Dan. Upon returning, bearing tear-stained dribble marks on both cheeks, he related, "First graders only get a talk." Crowding around our non-abused friend, the primary question surfaced, "Did he show you the electric paddle?" "No, but he told me he hoped he would never have to use it on me." Mortal fear governed our first grade behavior. Mr. N resigned at the end of my first grade year, and for the next 11 years two Methodist principals operated our school with amazing measures of grace.

The first day of first grade, Miss Olla announced, "Students with perfect attendance this year will receive a prize." This pronouncement sent off my mama's award syndrome. She became obsessed with my perfect attendance. One winter morning I awoke with "the bug," "big sick," "intestinal resistance sick," "trotting sick." Mama's nursing passion gave way to her forthcoming anticipated gleam at the award ceremony. I made roll call at 8:00 a.m. while mama waited outside the room to see if I was OK. Within the hour, my inability to retain the previous day's nourishment and thereby depositing a variety of semi-digested food elements on top of Miss Olla's foot resulted in medical liberation for the rest of the day.

At year's end, the Harmon twins and I each received a prize for perfect attendance. For some reason, Miss Olla insisted the twins not open their gift until they got home. She did encourage me to tear into my prize. Inside I found, to my great disappointment, one pair of striped ugly socks and a 5-cent Milky Way candy bar. For me, awards lost much of their attraction in the first grade. Besides, suspicion kicked in; I still wonder about the award the twins received.

First grade also contributed to the delinquency of my penmanship. I, the only left-handed child in the room, had to learn to write with my right hand. Miss Olla's rationale—she did not know how to teach writing to a left-handed person.

School as fun really began for me in the second and third grade. Our local school board hired Mrs. Ruffner, a kind, smiling, "my boys and girls," hugging, big lap teacher from Flora, Mississippi. The dear matron took her room and board at a local boarding house and rode the train back and forth, traveling to Flora each Friday and returning on Sunday nights. A well educated elementary teacher with a specialty in reading, she keenly graced me with a love for reading that prevails today. Looking back, I now see her vision for each of us, a vision we would share.

On the first day of class, she placed a mimeographed outline of a clown upon each desk. Each child, choosing his own greasy Crayola colors worked hard to stay in the lines of the clown's outline. Strangely, the clown's head pointed upward. Once the art project was finished, she tacked each clown in a row above the blackboard (chalkboard). Quite a colorful display. Next she moved over to our classroom library, books in a series of apple boxes covered in dust. She began dusting the books, reading the titles, and occasionally narrating the book's story. Now clowns upward-looking, books dusted and ready, she made her point—"This year we will read a lot." Each time a student finished a book, another title would be added to the clown's nose. He would juggle the books, and the three students who read the most books would receive an award at the end of the school year. Reaction! Oh, no, not this boy! I've been down that road before. It was a big-time turn off.

Unbeknown to all in the class, Mrs. Ruffner had selected a specific book for each student. My book, chosen by her, connected me to history for the rest of my life. Teacher intuition? God's grace? Both, I believe. Soon, book titles appeared and increased at a steady pace above my clown's nose. My reading fun displaced the memory of the first grade contest. Daily, students saw their advancement and a race continued throughout the year. I did receive one of the awards. You guessed it—another book. My award—a hard bound new copy of Daniel Defoe's *Robinson Crusoe*. While a bit advanced for a third grader, the story kept me busy reading over the summer of 1949, and I've been a reading nut ever since.

Aaron, today you can go online and quickly scan the short summary of almost any book. If so, you miss so much of the story and you rob yourself of a writer's gift. Read, read, read.

My trip going into and emerging out of the fourth and fifth grades has left me with a total absence of remembrance of academic development except for multiplication tables and long division. I do remember the teacher was the legendary Mrs. Earl C, a married lady with no children who maintained the capability of embarrassing kids who violated her code. Her wrath came upon me one cold, wet morning due to mud on my boots. After three trips to the basement to clean off the Mississippi gumbo mud, using only government thin toilet paper, she gave up for the day but constantly reminded me to "Stay out of the mud." Walking to and from school, I had no opportunity to walk on sidewalks. No sidewalks graced my route to and from school.

Her room, or our room, sat over the basement boiler and today OSHA would have condemned the hot and humid place. Sometimes during fifth grade, I developed my reputation for being tough. Playing football during recess, I ran the ball up through the line and took a hard lick to my right jaw. A permanent tooth jutted out, and blood flowed down and off my chin. I reached in my mouth, pulled out the dangling tooth, stuck the bicuspid in my pocket and played on, still bleeding. If you want points for being tough in the fifth grade, lose a tooth and play on, spittin' and wipin' blood. Instant initiation into tough.

A teacher for the sixth and seventh grades remained a town mystery up to the first day of school. As the 8:00 a.m. bell rang, a tall dark-complexioned man wearing a brown suit and carrying a handful of long switches entered the room. Hissing as he spoke, he told us his name and immediately gave orders to rearrange the room. His desk occupied the center spot. All student desks faced him in proximity to the length of the longest switch. He actually measured the distance from his seat through his long arm and on to the end of the sweet gum switches. Our large school house windows with no screens admitted flies. Mr. E's switches, though, had not been selected to swat flies. To the best of my memory, he never used a switch on a pupil. His bluff remained intact throughout the year. Each kid knew—he let me in here, and he can take me out.

Sometime during the sixth grade, M & M's candy came to our town. Their arrival preceded "Won't melt in your hand" times. During the winter of 1953, the class members seated close to the radiator conducted advanced chemical research with the pill-looking candy. The age, exposure to air, and color of any M & M could be determined by the amount of time and heat needed before the candy exploded and ran down the inside of the radiator. Soon, additional timed experiments produced warm chocolate candy passed clandestinely from student to student on toothpicks.

Once spring arrived, our chocolate delights resulted from further research. Hershey's cocoa and granulated sugar mixed together and packed into a snuff box made for a serious in school snack. Children fortunate enough to sit near a window could pack a lower lip and spit out the window. One boy earned the nickname "Snuff" sitting near a seventh grade window.

This letter may fall victim of the censor, resulting in a blah version. Oh well, school and fun came together mostly for our class of stalwart eradicators of ignorance. We learned from teachers who cared for kids, even with dirty boots. Great grace prevailed for the wide range of economic have and have-nots. Respect displaced fear of the faculty. "Mr." or "Mrs." always preceded a name. "Yes, Sir," "Yes, Ma'am" came from training at home. Misbehavior caught the attention of much of the town's people, and your reputation could afflict your entire school experience.

Aaron, today public education opportunities include an unheard term to me as a student—stress. I never became a victim of being taught for THE TEST. My teacher's paperwork was limited to a grade book and report cards. Class members took on some resemblance to a family, and, by the grace of God, nobody ever got LEFT BEHIND.

Eighth grade meant big time class changes and transition into high school. However, that's another story to be told later on.

Passing on values with hope,

Paw Paw

Comfort from Healing Graces

Rehoboth Hill
Cane Ridge, TN

Dear Aaron,

Big smiles and heavy tears of joy covered me over as I sat outside the hospital delivery room, even as you screamed your healthy first birth cry.

Immediately, pediatricians checked you over and pronounced, "healthy—fit for life." God's blessings of good health now give you continual growth and energy, and our whole family celebrates your wellness.

Aaron, a few anxious moments drew our attention, especially when you pushed an orange Crayola up your nose and later played the role of a "big boy" (age 5) as a kind doctor removed a fistula from your thumb. I am so thankful you have been privileged to enjoy excellent health and consistent good medical care provided by your mother, Mimi, and Paw Paw.

As you may by now guess, my childhood medical care showed little resemblance to the advances of medical science today.

Even though my Mother's Dad's accident interrupted her nurse's training, her practical knowledge kicked in to provide me care amidst childhood illness, health threats, and bumps and scrapes.

In our 1940's home, the first rule of health focused on cleanliness. Evidently, early on Mom bought into "Cleanliness is next to Godliness" (John Wesley. People think that's in the Bible. It's not; John Wesley said it.)

Mom elevated housekeeping, including washing, dusting, moping, waxing, disinfecting, and bathing, to a fine art. As a mother and wife, she declared our house a no dirt zone. Being clean meant looking clean, smelling clean, and feeling clean. Such an environment featured Pinesol, Duz, lye soap, Old Dutch Cleanser, real mops, brooms, dust rags, Johnson's Paste Wax,

Clorox, Oxydol, and of course Ivory Soap—"It floats." A germ had limited life-expectancy in our home on Munsterman Street.

One doctor, and only one—Dr. Sterling Kendall Johnson—blessed our town. Actually, I can only remember two others in the county. The town to this day has never included a hospital. Dr. Johnson performed limited surgeries at his house clinic in a room with a separate entrance. Actually, we had outpatient surgery 40 years before the big hospitals discovered the practice.

Dr. Johnson removed my tonsils one Monday morning, and Mom and Dad carried me home that afternoon (1945). In preparation for the procedure, Mom had prepared refrigerator ice cream. Playing the pain and agony to the hilt, I cried and cried for store-bought ice cream from Rhodes Drug Store. Softy Daddy gave in.

I do not think our town appreciated Dr. Johnson's medical skills as much as possible. He, a Roman Catholic in a Baptist/Methodist cult town, seemed used for his medical knowledge, but the community omitted him and his family from many local social affairs. He made house calls in the evenings. He knew the town like the back of his hand and responded quickly to emergencies phoned in, sometimes on six to eight party line telephones. I can even remember a few occasions waiting in his office as suddenly someone would rush in the door announcing a broken arm or a trauma that needed his immediate attention. Kindly he responded, "Mrs. Porch, I'll be back to take care of James in just a few minutes."

Old Dr. Johnson also encouraged home remedies, knowing many of his patients could not afford pills or drugstore elixirs, much less his bill. Medical specialists were at least 25 miles away in Jackson, and only on very rare occasions did our folk have the necessity, it seems, to seek them out. These were also the days when medical insurance was limited to a very few people. Local doctors sometimes went unpaid or provided medical care in exchange for farm goods or labor.

Our parents expected their children to contract a certain variety of illnesses including the big three—measles, mumps, and chicken pox. No vaccines existed to ward off these maladies. If by a certain age a child had not done time with the big three, some parents intentionally exposed children to the illnesses to get it over. I had five cousins living nearby. Our parents practiced exposure. So we played together and spent nights together until we experienced, in their estimation, adequate exposure. I vividly remember each of those maladies. The most frustrating one was measles. At that time prevailed a pronounced fear that measles would produce blindness unless your room remained dark. I remember all the shades were pulled down; no lights burned. Then one day, my Aunt Lucille bought me two new Roy Rogers funny books. Mom frequented the room of my illness, but I soon learned that if I took a flashlight and got under the covers, I could read the Roy Rogers comic books, absolutely assured I was going to go totally blind at any moment.

Among the other maladies were what we called "social diseases." These included lice and ring worm. According to one of my cousins, her Daddy killed a large wild turkey and each of us gathered the feathers and made Native American headbands. A few days later after intense itching, our mothers discovered the feathers were covered with lice. Naturally, our heads had become a lice haven. The eradication of lice in the 1940s resembled an experience that today would be conducted in an intensive care ward. As to ring worm, there are adults living today that bear scars from childhood of the microscopic little buggers that would get into the side of your head, eat out the tissue, and leave a scar.

And then, the feared diseases. Another cousin contracted scarlet fever, and I remember even as a child the anxious days as he labored to breathe under an oxygen tent. Actually, I contracted the same illness. However, my case was much less intense. Small pox had greatly been eradicated, but we still had to receive the inoculation. But the mother of all fears during the days of my childhood was polio. In summertime especially, great precautions including no swimming were taken to ensure that children would not in any way be exposed to the health threat. I vividly remember the summer of the announcement of the Salk vaccine and the new sense of security it gave to parents, as well as children, that the dreaded fear was over.

As mentioned earlier, because of an absence of insurance and limited income, home remedies usually preceded a doctor's visit and often provided sufficient healing cures. Neither of my parents smoked. Nevertheless, a bag of Red Man chewing tobacco held a central place in the bathroom medicine cabinet—especially from April through October—bee, wasp, and yellow jacket season. The process followed. A sting! A quick chew of tobacco! A soggy, yucky application of wet spit saturated tobacco! Hear me now—almost instant cure! Mississippi's afflictions also included poison oak and poison ivy. As to remedy, two profound treatments gave an itching child a choice. 1) Cut open a red ripe tomato and rub the fresh juice all over the itching area. Later apply mayonnaise and lick it off. Actually, omit the mayonnaise; I just hate to waste good tomatoes. 2) Using a sharp razor blade, shave a bar of lye soap (octagon soap) into a black skillet with a small amount of water. Make a paste and apply the concoction to the itchy area. Itching will transition into screaming, and once the paste is removed the hair pulls loose, also. Yet, it works!

Warts, seed warts! Big, unattractive growths limiting one's social acceptance and a cause of various attempts at eradication. Sulfuric acid applied with a cotton swab provided the best removal measure for a wart. Somehow word got around my high school that I could cure warts. Practicing totally without the benefit of a license, I spent many recess periods cloistered away in the chemistry room applying the acid elixir to fellow students and faculty alike. Oh my, what liability! I suppose the town's school board, county commission, Mississippi Board of Education, governor, and United States Department of Education could have borne the brunt of an ascending liability lawsuit. But remember, I was a mere teenager of the age of President Harry Truman who practiced "The buck stops here."

In those days, many people could be trusted to maintain discipline with medicines that today cannot be administered except by professional medical personnel under strict controlled measures.

Any citizen of our town could purchase one ounce of Paregoric simply by payment and signing his name to the pharmacist's register. Numerous small children gained relief from a variety of discomforts by a very small drop applied to the tongue. This dangerous medicine, an opium derivative, if used, demanded the experienced counsel of parents or grandparents whose children had lived through and thrived after a dose of Paregoric.

As you know, Paw Paw's Daddy earned his keep and family income as a blacksmith. His calling to work with fire, hot iron, wrenches, hammers, and sharp-edged tools resulted in many cuts, scrapes, punctures, and other bodily harm. Dad limited his healing arsenal to three items: coal oil, rubbing alcohol, and turpentine. He cleansed the wound with isopropyl alcohol, poured on coal oil (kerosene), wrapped the wound, and resumed work. I remember cuts that today would demand stitches and possibly other treatment measures including antibiotics. No time! He had work in process. No money! He medicated by a previously used cure. It had worked! The wound would heal! Personally, Dad applied coal oil to many of my childhood cuts, scrapes, skinned knees, and abrasions. Somehow, coal oil always relieved the soreness. I'll omit commentary on turpentine as further discussion would require reference to delicate anatomical applications beyond the sensitivity of a religious book.

I suppose an entire book could be written, and has been written, concerning home remedies that have sustained individuals and families, literally for centuries. I hope, though, a few of these insights will help you understand a different time and how we made it through in the midst of some traumas.

Our age also, as today, included medicines with questionable reputations. Over in Louisiana in the 1950s, a gentleman by the name of Dudley LeBlanc concocted an elixir that he named Hadacol. A joke resulted—"he had to call it something." Actually, he was a member of the Louisiana legislature and evidently had a real knack for making money. His miracle medicine caught on all over the South. Advertisements on billboards, radio, and in newspapers promised cures for practically anything. The medicine even prompted the writing of a popular country music song entitled "Hadacol Boogie." Large white 18-wheel trucks moved back and forth across the states of the South carrying hundreds of gallons of Hadacol to grocery stores, pharmacies, convenience stores, country stores, and any store that would stock the medicine. Hadacol came in a variety of sized bottles. Actually, the tonic included a large amount of alcohol. Many Mississippians living in a dry state took advantage of this medicine for an expanded variety of maladies. My Aunt Lollie considered Hadacol to be a gift from God. Other potent and promising medicines included Pepticon, Carter's Little Liver Pills, and Blunt's Hair Tonic guaranteed to turn gray hair to black or grow hair on bald heads. Usually, information on most tonics focused on the ability of the medicine to bring new health to the liver. My best guess is if your liver is out of whack, you've got trouble all over. Finally, no article on home remedies in my house would be complete without reference to Dr. Caldwell's Sienna Laxative, Black Draught, and Three Sixes. I am thankful that time and space will not permit me to comment any further on these last three. Each of them reaches beyond my desire to reminisce.

Some readers may wonder why I select some of these subjects. Yes, they are big parts of my life. They narrate an age that is gone and will never return—as no age ever returns. They are indeed part of a legacy that I protect. Yet the overwhelming rationale I keep coming back to is this— God enabled me and our family to make it through hard times. There were many measures of grace, I believe, that He even used though some may be the subject of scoffers in this post-modern age. And after all, there may be some real merit in these writings because, who knows, we may have another hard time.

Passing on values with hope,

Paw Paw

Ready, Batter?

Rehoboth Hill
Cane Ridge, TN

Dear Aaron,

One June day, late in the afternoon, I came home from baseball practice noticeably bearing a bad attitude and grumpy disposition.

We called our baseball "Little League," but not in the official way with all the rules, uniforms, and registered bats. Our field, the old abandoned high school football field, had been made playable only by the hard work, sweat, cuts, scratches, and nicks of some 15-20 boys including your Paw Paw. We began the process by pleading with Mr. Rutledge, the school principal, for permission to use the old abandoned field. He, a friend to all of us, in turn talked the town board of aldermen into their support. That meant no help, no money—just the privilege for the boys to clean up an overgrown patch of weeds, junk, briars, and we wondered what else. Our local school property included a powerful Yazoo Master Mower, the undisputed prince of lawn mowers in the 1950s. In total confession, the mower, "borrowed" from the basement of the high school, stayed hidden at my house for a week. My dad, Big Milton, never knew our place housed temporary confiscated school and government property. J.C.'s dad owned the Shell station, a ready source of 29 cents a gallon gasoline. Everybody able took turns pushing or pulling the heavy old belt-driven mower. My blacksmith expertise came in handy having access to files and knowing how to sharpen the blade.

After several days of hard work, the tall weeds and grass had surrendered to the mower and the academic property had been returned safely to the school basement.

Bill's mamma owned several chicken houses, but I never knew for sure where the web wire came from for the back stop. Living across the street from the old field, I volunteered with Dad's permission shovels, rakes, hoes, posthole digger, hammer, staples, and wire stretcher. Our group spent many hot hours trying to level off the infield. One day, Dad, having observed our work become misery and frustration, came over to offer a suggestion, "You boys need to drag that field or you'll never get it smoothed out." "Good idea, but how?" He seemed prepared for our puzzle. "Come over to my shop. We'll build a drag." In a short time, with his directions, we nailed several rough 2 x 10, 12-foot long oak pieces of lumber together for a heavy drag. One boy named "Alec" for smart-alec, asked if we could pull the drag with our bicycles. Dad helped out again, "Boys, line up along that drag, pick it up, and let's go to the field." While struggling, wobbling, and often resting, we steadily moved toward the field. He drove on ahead of us in our family's old 1951 Cambridge turquoise Plymouth. Once we met him on the dry rough field, he chained the drag to the frame of the car and told us all to sit down on the drag and hold on. For the next hour or so, he drug us and the 2 x 10s around and around while we ate dust, fell off, climbed back on, laughed, pushed, and shoved, all the time knocking down bumps and filling in low places.

Occasionally throughout that summer, "Mr. Milton" would come back over to drag the field. Along about the drag time, somebody remembered that our town had fielded a baseball team back before World War II. The barber shop talk brought to mind the question, "Whatever happened to the home plate, bats, catcher's mitt, and baseballs?" Discussion spread across town and turned to searching and discovery. For well over a decade, that equipment had been awaiting a bunch of kids. Reflecting back on that entire process, I learned a lesson. The equipment did not appear until the field was prepared.

As many of us had chores, we played our first actual practice game late one afternoon. By then, the group of players had increased so two entire teams could take the field. That same afternoon we used the time-honored method of juvenile team selection. Two boys chose up sides. Each team made position assignments, and that's when my attitude went sour. My team leader sent me to right field. Right field! After all that hard work and even assistance from my Daddy! Right field meant standing in the heat, shifting weight back and forth, swatting gnats, and knowing nobody except by accident hit to right field, even a foul ball. Even running out there on the field brought an embarrassment to my athletic skills and the forthcoming jeers, "Porch plays right field." And so by the time I got home,

I was ready to quit and enjoy my pity party because of the team leader's lack of appreciation for my athletic ability.

Dad's question broke the dam on my pent up anger, "How'd the game go?" My immediate answer showed intense feeling, "I had to play right field." His reply—"So?" His unappreciative disposition unleashed a barrage of my pity and anger.

Once I finished, he waited to add to my frustration. Finally, he spoke looking directly at me, "Son, even in right field you do get to bat."

Passing on values with hope,

Paw Paw

"Get 'r done" Necessity

Rehoboth Hill
Cane Ridge, TN

Dear Aaron,

A friend graced me with a "Git 'r done" cap. My proud possession daily reminds me of my family's work ethic. While holding no claim to inventing the term, the Porch boys, Charlie, Henry, John, Ed, and Milton (my Daddy), and the Barnes sisters, Maude, Vera, Ester, Lucille, Ola, Bessie, Clara, Louise, and Lillian (my Mother) practiced with discipline that very southern labor principle nearly a century before caps and tee-shirts and comedy lowered the work value to the red-neck dictionary.

Simply stated, git 'r done means finish the job. These five blacksmith boys and nine farm girls carried over into adulthood the lesson of individual responsibility to complete their work. Most blacksmith and farm jobs in 1900, and even into the 1950s, demanded beginning and finishing a specific task. Each hoed out her own row. Each built his wagon wheels from the hub out to the tire. They had to finish on time. The absence of material or a broken tool never afforded a legitimate excuse. A living, or livelihood, depended on completing work. Even on-the-job injuries at our house only merited the first-aid of rubbing alcohol and coal oil (kerosene).

My mental picture remembrances of my folks' work appear radically different from today's generation as daily work now represents segments of labor far removed from the total task.

Corporate management thrives on the yo-yo effect of paper up or paper down channels. Medical practitioners often promote a restricted specialty and show little, if any, embarrassment to relying on, "That's not my specialty." Church health suffers from ministers, committees, and congregations who seldom venture beyond the box of a job description or assignment. And, God abundantly bless the millions of factory workers whose willingness

90

to be restricted to an assigned labor force enables finished products to contribute to my life needs each day.

In order to climb down from this soap box, I give in to reminiscing over a season when git 'r done kept Faith with its original meaning, and as a worker I discovered the joy in finishing well.

Near the end of my sixth grade school year, Dad casually remarked, "We (meaning he and I) need to do some work on the front porch." Whatever you're named for should bear witness to good maintenance and eye appeal.

Looking over the porch, I saw a few rotten planks, a sagging front step, one leaning post, and a floor needing paint. For me, this was no big job. I heard "repairs." A few days later, having pondered the true condition of the front gallery functionally, structurally, and aesthetically, Dad announced "we" would lower the entire porch, build a form around the exterior, dig a footing, build a block wall for underpinning, pour a concrete slab, and add brick steps. He meant renovation. Today, such a project would demand a stand-around foreman, two framing carpenters, at least two concrete masons, one brick mason, a painter, and a Ready-Mix concrete delivery, all operating on the schedule—"whenever we arrive" to "until we knock off early."

Back to 1951. My family's limited financial condition was never a secret. Dad and Mamma believed that all members of the family should bear unity because of limited money. And so I wondered, "How would we pay for the project?"

Dad planned ahead. You did not survive The Great Depression by spontaneity. So we began gathering material. We hauled bucket after bucket after bucket of sand from the town creek to the house in the trunk of our 1941 Super Deluxe Chevrolet. His home church, Rehoboth, had removed four concrete block walls due to foundation problems, and each saved block was being sold for 10 cents. Uncle Charlie, head deacon of the church, hauled the blocks for us and collected. Dad, over the years, had saved up all 4 x 4s and 4 x 6 pieces left over from building pulp wood truck beds. Now, the next material is a bit tricky to narrate. Mr. Milton negotiated a truck load of masonry sand and a truck load of pea gravel through an often-elected county government official in exchange for sharpening county road grater blades and cutting and sharpening a mass of bridge pins. Remember, this was the 1950s, and government served the people. My legal research confirms the statute of limitations has expired pertaining to such endeavors.

The actual git 'r done task commenced early one April morning (our school year lasted only eight months).

Standing in front of the porch holding two sharpened hand saws, Dad described the first step of the process. Handing me a saw he said, "You are left-handed, so go to the north end of the porch. I'm right-handed, so I'll saw from the south end. We'll saw to meet in the middle." We literally sawed off the porch by hand to provide a deck on which to pour concrete. From that point, we worked off and on when he had time away from the blacksmith shop. The two of us cleaned old mortar from the blocks, lowered the porch, reset pillars, dug the footing, mixed mortar, and laid blocks I carried and he set. Once we built the form around the porch, we prepared to pour the slab. Right about that time, Mamma set the date to finish our work, July 4th. I think that's the first time Dad ever offered me premarital counseling, "Son, if Mamma's happy, it's a good work." I had already begun to fear, dread, and even cry thinking about pouring the slab—all of which had to be completed by hand in one day.

God hears a child's weeping. A few days before the pouring, an African-American concrete mason, a good friend of Dad's, came by the shop to pick up some sharpened plow points. Sam Hobson asked, "Big Milton, how are you and Little Milton gonna mix that concrete?" Daddy answered, "By hand." Sam grinned and said, "I ain't paid you yet for these plows, so why don't I just come by with my mixer and the boys the day you want it poured?" At that moment, as a very young teenager, I knew profoundly the purpose of *The Doxology*. Sam and his three fine boys worked as a concrete and masonry team with us a few days later, and by noon we "got 'r done."

And so I'll deviate a bit from my original premise. I came to believe when you work faithfully to git 'r done, God may just send you some help to finish the job. Maybe the missionary apostle's testimony, "I have finished the course" (II Timothy 4:7) set the Christian precedent to git 'r done.

Passing on values with hope,

Paw Paw

Christmas, Plain and Simple

Rehoboth Hill
Cane Ridge, TN

Dear Aaron,

My home town observed a consensus of respect, an unwritten but accepted understanding that no public signs of Christmas appeared prior to Thanksgiving Day.

Christmas, the Christian season, affirmed the One Almighty God who invaded our world as a baby in a far away place a long time ago to give us peace, joy, and hope through His grace. This sentence offers no definition of Christmas. Instead, the attempt declares my observation of the majority of folk where I grew up. I have no intention to label my hometown as a place of sainthood. Actually, some of the Christian acceptance of Christmas sadly was an assumption. Still, I cherish through memories the belief I can build a strong case for the many who believed in the dignity and even power of the season.

I grew up in the last self-regulated generation before rampant commercialism of Christmas won out. To a large degree, the season in the 40s and 50s possessed a simplicity and reverence that is tragically lost now in the 21st century. My memories, some recorded here, remain precious and filled with hope as I offer you at least a glimpse of Christmas in another time. Maybe, my mind-pictures will cause you to wonder about a different yuletide when *giving* won out over *getting*.

Any attempt to memorialize the season 50-60 years ago as an era of the best and proper observance is lost in my confession announcing our first sign of Christmas arriving in the mail—the *Western Auto Christmas Catalogue*. Mailed locally, probably the Friday after Thanksgiving, every kid awaited the wish book. How coincidental! By Saturday, go-to-town day, Mr. Pat had totally transformed his store into a haven of toy hope.

Actually, the collection only included one of each advertised item. To the best of my memory, on that special Saturday you looked and pointed while clutching a parent's hand as they kept telling you, "Don't touch Mr. Pat's stuff." He sold only a few items early in December. Maybe a town ordinance or community tradition gave everybody the opportunity to see first and buy later. Gradually other stores added enough decorations to admit Christmas was coming but still a month away.

Our town boasted of only one electric stop light—at the corner of highway 80 and Brooks Street. Early in the 1950s, the board of mayor and aldermen sanctioned garlands of red and green lights at the intersection. The following Sunday, the before Bible lesson gossip in the TEL class at the Baptist church focused on, "The town's gone gaudy." Once some families began stringing lights outside their houses, especially blinking lights, the gossip grew to "vulgar" and "honky-tonk." Meanwhile, at the Pelahatchie Consolidated School, kids including myself reveled at the opportunity to draw and color Christmas images on Blue Horse notebook paper and paste them on schoolroom windows. Christmas indeed was on the way.

As to home decorations, we cut a live tree from Mrs. Barrow's land. Dad had her permission to cut one cedar tree each year. And so, as father and son we made the search together for the appropriate evergreen. Once the tree was up, necessity ruled that each light had to be checked very carefully. Any one blown bulb could short out the entire set of 12 lights. We never owned bubble lights, even though I always admired them. One year we upgraded the decorations to include a simple non-blinking electric star for the top of the tree. Arranging the nativity scene took on a spirit of reverence. Positioned on a square table with turn-screw legs, the Holy scene occupied a prominent place in the family living room. The tabletop covered with cotton batting became a soft background to nestle the stable and Holy Night participants. While Mary and Joseph, the shepherds and wisemen appeared in various positions over the years, Baby Jesus' place always received center stage. As I write this letter, my joy mixes with a loss as I wonder whatever happened to that precious piece of my Christmas past, the manger scene. I hold on to the hope that someday I'll enjoy a delightful discovery somewhere in the packed up Porch stuff.

As I recall, our home was decorated each year through Christmas 1959. Dad died in the spring of 1960, Mom moved to Mississippi College as campus nurse, and we were away from the home for quite some time. During the Christmas school break of 1960, she and I went back home to a cold house that had been vacant for months and bore no signs of celebrations. Dad's absence at that Christmas time left a void, an emptiness, and big room for much grief. On Christmas morning around 9:30 a.m., my Aunt Lucille drove up, came in the house and point-blank said, "You are eating Christmas dinner with us." Actually, her family had not even opened any presents when we arrived. They shared presents with Mom and me. We had none for them. It is a Christmas that I remember so vividly because all we had to offer was, "Thank you," our smiles, our tears, and our hugs for being remembered by family and being just a receiver. Until that Christmas, I never understood how much Dad's presence meant to our family. Even the year before while Dad was quite ill and bedridden, Mom and I shared Christmas together with him—our last Christmas together.

We went to the Baptist church house quite often during the Christmas season. Each Wednesday night and Sunday night the choir gathered for cantata practice. Our church moved into the era of the Christmas cantata one year after the Methodists pioneered the musical event. Actually, the Methodists purchased the town's first electronic Baldwin organ. During the following year, the Baptist church countered by purchasing a Hammond organ. I think this detail is correct, for I could never remember which organ—Hammond or Baldwin—had the slide stops and the other had the flip stops. The Methodist cantata thing, involving Baptist youth, came about through the aggressive efforts of Rev. Willard. His intentions were to enlist, not to recruit. Possibly the venture of an involvement of the two denominational groups into one cantata hastened the buying of the Baptist organ. My most vivid recollection of a specific cantata was the one entitled *Love Transcending*. At one point in the musical message Mr. Billy, our town's 5' 2" train depot agent, rose to his point of grandeur with a one word solo, "Glory." Among other musical highlights was the annual experience of singing *O Holy Night*. I never understand why we reserve that beautiful hymn to just a few days of the year.

Well, Aaron, I suppose you're wondering if Santa Claus existed in the 40s and 50s. Emphatically, yes! I remember three special Santa Claus gifts—a B.B. gun, a cap pistol, and my new bicycle. Dad had been in the VA Hospital in Jackson for over two months before Christmas one year. Each Saturday, Mom and I visited him enjoying the opportunity to have lunch together in the hospital canteen. The facility included a store providing items for the patient's needs. For some reason, the collection included toys.

Week after week, I saw the same cap pistol set complete with holster and belt, and I reminded Mom and Dad that Christmas was soon to arrive. Evidently, Santa Claus made his way by the VA Hospital because on Christmas morning the cap pistol set appeared under the tree. My second well remembered gift (the B.B. gun) conjures up special memories of that Christmas day. Actually, I had the flu and could not go outside and play or even get out of bed. Dad was determined, though, that I enjoy that B.B. gun. He went outside my bedroom window, hung a cowbell by a string on a tree, removed the screen, raised the window, and let me shoot at the dangling cowbell through the window. All day long, our neighbors heard the ping when I hit the bell.

My final well remembered gift was the bicycle. For some unknown reason, Santa Claus left the bicycle unassembled, and years later Mom told me Dad spent much of the night assembling the bicycle and attempted to ride it through the house. Evidently, the blessing of being a deep sleeper prevented me from knowing what was going on. I wish today I could remember exactly the Christmas Dad joined together with Santa Claus and made many of my gifts. He designed a rocky horse made out of car springs with the head of a horse painted on a piece of wood. I also recall a self propelled go-cart with the speed determined by my ability to push and pull the handles. My Christmas morning began not by going immediately to the tree. First, Dad or Mom would go to make sure that Santa Claus had been there and everything was ready. I can still see the glow of those red, green, and white lights reflected against the floral wallpaper and providing just enough light to reveal to me what miraculous treasures arrived over the night. Those moments of discovery in the dim haze of the lights and the smell of the cedar tree hold a fresh place in my memory.

And yes, we ate well. The enticing smells of Christmas cooking bore testimony to good happenings in the kitchen. Cooking, according to my Mamma, was much more than mixing ingredients and applying the degreed amount of heat for the specified time. Mom cooked off the recipe. A list of contents and instructions only provided her a beginning. Her creativity, inspired by risk and the sense of "It ought to be about right," dominated every dish.

No turkey ever invaded our kitchen. Turkeys had to be bought. Our meat was a combination of green ham and baked hen. The hen, preferred over turkey anyhow, made better dressing. The green ham existed years before

Dr. Seuss. Mamma initiated the tradition of boiling and baking a fresh (or green) ham as an annual cooking gift to my Dad. Our Christmas also included an ample amount of fresh turnip greens. I've never attended any Christmas dinner in any other place that included turnip greens. How sad to neglect such a delicacy. I suppose it was just a Porch thing. All our Christmas sweets included pecans. Our house sat in the middle of four gigantic pecan trees that bore bushels upon bushels of nuts each year. My overindulgence in pecan pies in my growing up years caused me to lose an appreciation for the southern delicacy until just a few years ago. Mom's pecan recipes also included a burnt sugar caramel candy that required much preparation and, on occasion, failure. This was her take-to-church candy, and I have seen her remake the entire recipe if the sweet treat failed to have the smoothness and texture she expected. The only dish requiring ingredients purchased at Goodman's Grocery Store was ambrosia—fresh oranges, a fresh pineapple, a fresh coconut, and a bottle of maraschino cherries. All of these ingredients had to be cut by hand and properly mixed. Ambrosia in my hometown was entirely a Baptist dish due to the fact that we lived in a dry state. There could never be any Episcopalian invasion of ingredients.

With the exception of the year I had the influenza, our Christmas day always included the annual pilgrimage to Mamma's childhood home at Barefoot Springs in Rankin County, Mississippi. Her family included nine girls and two boys. All now grown and married, they gathered on Christmas day back at the place of their beginnings and sent the grandchildren a very strong sense of family as together we gathered to eat, to laugh, to cry, to get on each other's nerves, and once again enjoy the hugs of family folk. A few years ago, prior to Mom's death, I realized my Grandmother and Grandfather's house never included any decorations. My Mother indicated there was no money for decorations as they were growing up, and usually Christmas meant either an apple or an orange, or a stick of candy for each child. In the absence of the decorations, though, the family gathered together to provide its own festivity in the human spirit. We bore together a growing and abiding understanding that our togetherness only happened because of Jesus' birth. The one exception to the absence of decoration was in my Grandmother's gumdrop cake. She baked from scratch a cake covered over by a crusty white frosting. Weeks before, she would have requested one of the kids to bring home some small colored gumdrops. Late in the morning just before we all gathered to eat,

Grandmamma carefully placed those colored gumdrops on the white icing. It seemed to me a picture of color in the snow.

Aaron, this whole letter has been about remembering. I've tried to take you on a trip back through my years with a sense of mission—you even today are a part of that story back there, even though you will only know it through memories shared with you. There are many other parts of this big story, and maybe one day I can tell you more.

Aaron, pack up your memories along the way. Take time to remember and keep in mind that these memories will be a big part of who you are and become. All of what I've tried to say in this letter focuses on moving toward the day of Christmas celebration. Actually in a few hours, Christmas day becomes a let-down in relation to the planning and preparation for the season. Soon the event begins to fade away. Maybe as Christians we just allow this to happen to us, and it is our own fault.

Our Christ one day ascended to the Father, and now we await His reappearing. Keeping the hope in mind as we work back to the point of exclamation by the angel, "Today, in the City of David there has been born for you a Savior who is Christ the Lord," we can better understand that Christmas ought to be celebrated each day. Once born, that day—that real day—ought to be every day. He is born, and life has never been the same. The memories of Christmas are a big part of what Christmas ought to be about. To God be the glory.

Passing on values with hope,

Paw Paw

Check Out Your Balcony

Rehoboth Hill
Cane Ridge, TN

Dear Aaron,

In addition to my mamma and daddy, I grew up in the presence of some life-changing folk. That term, a conveyed tag of endearment, pointed to persons who over time and through observation received the respect of the community, mostly for living in behalf of others.

In another way of speaking, real Christian virtues came through the way people lived their appointed days. Designations such as role models, examples, or influencers stopped way short of the honor due these special sons and daughters. Now for me, they sit in my gallery, or balcony, and join others in my "encompassing cloud of witnesses" (Hebrews 12:1). In a revered sense, I call each of them a cheerleader. All now are assuredly citizens of the Kingdom of Heaven and continue to bear influence upon my life as each by the grace of God appeared right on time during turning point seasons of my childhood and teen years. I hold as precious, memories of words spoken or character actions never erased by death. During life's crossroad moments, I have reached back for their counsel. Now their importance exceeds even my memory. Assuredly my Heavenly Father allows one or more from time to time to be my angel unaware.

Dr. S.K. Johnson and Miss Mamie Kincaid, physician and nurse, attended my birth. The difficult delivery, ultimately a Caesarean, occurred under a gloomy shadow of death. Mom had lost twins two years earlier. According to an inscription in my baby book, Miss Mamie shouted to Dr. Johnson, "This baby must live!" Quickly she arranged two large pans side by side— one filled with warm water, the other containing iced water. Utilizing an old midwife way, she alternated in immersing the newborn me in warm and cold water until I began to breathe.

Having no insurance, Daddy paid cash for my delivery. Dr. S.K.'s bill totaled $1,000.10. Dad believed the dime recorded the cost of the ice.

Dr. Johnson drove fast, took Thursday afternoons off to fish (a no-no in our town), and shuffled his feet constantly. In his office behind the drugstore, he cared for his patients with kind hands, maintained an antiseptic environment, and often to the dismay of the druggist next door prescribed home remedies knowing most folks had little money. He cared for me from birth through a rusty nail puncture, siege of scarlet fever, and a tonsillectomy. I still see him driving up to our house in his two-toned blue Buick. Dr. Johnson made house calls.

As a son of Pelahatchie, I spent 12 of my 18 years in one school house. Going into ninth grade, I discovered arithmetic transitioned into algebra, and numbers and letters got mixed up in weird ways. My only salvation came through a dear lady called out of retirement to fill in for the regular teacher who became ill. This kind, disciplined algebra master had actually taught my mother 20 years earlier. Her blessing to me extended far beyond mathematics.

One day, taking a shortcut past her garage, I noticed stacks and stacks of magazines inside the little building. The next day at school, I mustered up enough courage to ask Mrs. Summer, "May I borrow some of the old copies of *Life, Look, Collier's*, and *Saturday Evening Post* out in your garage?" In a smile response, she offered me free rights to borrow and return any of the collection. Our cathedral Philco radio suffered from chronic static, we couldn't afford a newspaper or telephone, and television had not reached our town. Those magazines offered me a paper and picture road out of my home town and literally into the culture and news world as regularly I borrowed and returned a weekly stack over a period of several years.

Mr. J.O. served as our school principal beginning my second grade year. The short, balding, disciplined, Methodist layman carried two watches— one to begin the school day and the other to dismiss classes at the end of the day. He took in late and let out early. During the summer after my eighth grade year, I hired on as his garden boy. One of my most memorable jobs required sticking three rows of butterbeans. Evidently, I did not pay attention to his directions. That afternoon he stopped by the house and, wearing a wide grin, announced for the whole family, "James, you stuck my peas." No anger, rather a joke on me. Years later he still kidded me about pole climbing purple hull peas. The point? He simply understood a mistake and saw no need to press shame down on a careless kid. Over his principal years, he conducted numerous behavior modifications upon many students. I cannot recall any student being shamed by the gracious little man.

While church attendance never became an option, church enjoyment took on great meaning through the life and witness of Knox, Elizabeth, and Bill. In another Paw Paw letter, I offered a tribute to Knox, my boyhood Sunday School teacher.

Elizabeth, wife of an invalid husband dependent upon her for all his needs, still made time for a group of rowdy R.A. boys each Monday afternoon at 3:30 p.m., usually on the front steps of the Baptist church (weather permitting). Those great days of Southern Baptist activity took on value to me as she told stories of Baptist leaders and missionaries and their ministry for Christ.

Bill held counsel regularly every Sunday night for youth Training Union. We read or gave assigned parts and discovered Baptist polity and manners of doing church. Some, maybe much of that stuff, stuck and has shaped my grasp of true Baptist life.

One day, John Cook moved his family to town. He soon began talking up Boy Scouts of America to our parents. In a matter of weeks, Troop 66, composed of 21 fellows age 11 and up, began gathering at City Hall for meetings and sessions in camp craft. Mr. John's wisdom extended to a wide expanse of patience in pushing us beyond our own self-expectations. While honoring our local culture, he challenged the troop to attempt big goals.

On another day, I joined the 4-H Club for one reason. Each meeting provided an excused absence from English class. I never intended on even meeting the county leader, J.W. Terry. By the way, Aaron, your mother is named for him. Once the club railroaded me into an elected office, he responded with a handwritten note of congratulations. Such a gesture got my attention and initiated a bond that gave me a confidence in myself that through Christ matures even today.

Joe Walter Terry lived to link his character to his life investment—youth. His exceptionally wide range of knowledge included animal nurture, crop development, parliamentary procedure, public speaking, citizenship, gardening, and community development—all focused toward cultivating a spirit of self-achievement in boys. He dared me to push out my own envelope and constantly maintained his rare witness, never to solve my dilemmas but rather point me to examine options and own my own decisions. A Baptist deacon and a government employee, but even more a realist, Mr. Terry's life came over to me with a genuineness of interest in my life exceeded only by my parents.

These rare people, exemplary of others, all teachers in various dimensions, taught me for a time beyond my childhood and youth years. In such tutorial exercises, they extended their faith. Each, an investor, sought no return. No wonder now over half a century later I hold in my heart a sense of their abiding presence.

Aaron, who's going to sit in your balcony? You will make the choices. Select intentionally. Allow no one in by default.

Passing on values with hope,

Paw Paw

Critter-Friends Demand Respect

Rehoboth Hill
Cane Ridge, TN

Dear Aaron,

Ought - A very appropriate word for kids, as in "Children ought to grow up around animals." Oh, I can go on and on telling you why I believe my own conviction. Better still, I'll just tell you about some of my dogs, incidents with a horse, and an ordeal with a raccoon.

Jackie Boy, part shepherd and otherwise, beat me into the family. Photos taken in my toddler years often included my pleasant-faced long-haired protector. According to Mama, he took an early liking to me and patiently endured my slobbering, pulling hair, and crawling over his back. As Daddy's dog originally, he had learned his tenderness from the calloused hands of the blacksmith, quite probably a preparation to become my first canine friend. Sometime shortly after my fourth birthday, Jackie Boy suddenly disappeared. Sadly, Mama explained, "He got sick and died." Years later, far from my remembrance, Mama told me I cried and watched from the front bedroom window so sure he would come back. Ten years later, her story continued. A strange and angry dog had wandered through town. He growled, snapped, attacked, and bit several neighborhood dogs. Before anyone realized his condition, the bad dog bit my Jackie Boy. Shortly, a tame, gentle, caring friend changed into a growling, vicious, dangerous animal. Now rabid, Daddy had to destroy my pet. Even hearing the truth years later, I felt my loss. My pictures with him help hold on to the good times in early years.

And then came Blue and Brownie. One summer afternoon, a very tired and sad looking lady dog wandered into our back yard. Mama, seeing the old dog through the kitchen window, rushed outside to warn me not to pet the animal. Sensing as only a mother could, she explained, "She's hungry and about to have pups." Quickly preparing a bowl of scraps heavy with meat gravy and a bowl of water (all our dogs must have been allergic to dog food), she fed the long-legged shepherd. Mom violated Daddy's dictum, "Feed a stray dog once and you've got a dog." A few mornings later, we began hearing squeaking sounds from under the house. Daddy and I crawled under the house, and near the chimney base we found two blind puppies and their mother very weak, and according to Dad, she was dying. I carried the puppies out. Gently as possible, my father brought the mama dog out from under the house. She died that afternoon. Now, inheriting two blind, hungry infant puppies, I began learning the gift of caretaking—a welcome label I wear today and will wear all my life. Once their eyes opened, the pups (one brown and white the other literally colored dark blue) began moving around much to my enjoyment. The brown and white pup, limited by a lame back leg, received my special attention and affection. After supper one evening, Dad and I each carried a bowl of food to the pups. Unknown to Mom, Dad, or me, a small ball of dough accidentally had gotten into one bowl—the one for Brownie.

Gobbling up his food, Brownie choked on the dough ball. Immediately, Dad tried to dislodge the obstruction. All effort only seemed to wedge the dough further into the puppy's throat. By my Dad's tears, I knew his hurt. The tragedy even exceeded Mom's nursing skills. Even now, I can remember the stress in the puppy's eyes, his little body quivering, the seeming sadness of his brother, Blue, and our family's growing grief as my innocent little furry friend stopped breathing. Wisely, Mom picked up Blue and she and Dad went into the house, leaving me along with the dead puppy. Sometime later, she and Dad described my self-consoling act of caressing and talking to Brownie. Then sensing the right time, Dad came out, picked me up, hugged me tight, and whispered, "Why don't we bury him next to his Mommy?" We did. My loss, my grief, my helping dig a grave that day hit me hard with the reality of seeing death happen. Now, 60 years later, having seen the death of very close loved ones and friends, the pain has not diminished. I really hope I never lose the pain of a loss by death. Such would deny the real me.

Okay. Now for the horse stuff. In another letter I introduced Strutter, the on-loan, contract-for-riding in return for pasture rights horse. One day Strutter saved my life. Another day Daddy saved me from laming or abusing the kind equine.

As best remembered, I saddled and trotted her up our driveway, tugged the left rein to ride down Methodist Church Hill and on over to the Davis brothers' house.

Suddenly Stutter shot out both front feet and threw me against the saddle horn, burying my face in her mane. Irritated, I raised up, felt the quiver travel the length of her back and looking ahead saw the reason for her stall. A gigantic rattlesnake, seemingly as long as the width of the road, leisurely slithered across and into the ditch and weeds.

Strutter had smelled the snake, stopped quickly, and prevented an encounter that by snake bite could have killed her and by fright alone would have messed me up big time. Two hours later, a rattlesnake 5' 10" long was killed coming out of that same field a block away, assuredly the same snake.

As earlier declared, my Father had little patience with any abuse—human and/or animal.

One horrid, hot August afternoon I opted out of boredom by challenging Strutter to climb a high sloping bank in sight of our house. Once successfully still in the saddle and on top, I tried out her skills traveling down the bank. The test ride over, I kept on riding up and down totally oblivious to the overheating, winding, and lathering of my friend.

Daddy had been watching. Apparently hoping I would stop but uncertain, he, unknown to me, sauntered over from the house. Coming down the bank, I saw him bearing a most unkind expression—a combination of anger and disappointment. He spoke direct and quiet, "Climb off and unsaddle Strutter. Walk her slowly back to the house. Carry the saddle and meet me in the shop."

Once the scheduled shop meeting began, he spoke again, holding a piece of plow line in his hand. "I'm gonna whip you, and I don't believe you'll ever abuse a horse again." He did! I haven't! Enough said! Lesson learned!

As to the raccoons, I'll attempt brevity. My uncle caught two raccoons and kept them in a strong cage in preparation for a July 4 volunteer fire department fund raiser called "Coon on a Log." A raccoon dog would swim out to a log floating in the lake and attempt to pull the raccoon chained to the log off into the water. Money was raised by registration fees. Usually, the raccoon won to the embarrassment of the dog and his owner.

In the weeks prior to the event, the raccoon cages located out behind my uncle's icehouse became a daily attraction to me and my cousin. Over days of feeding, touching them through the welded wire, talking gently with the furry guys, we decided (against all dire warnings never to open the cages) that gentleness prevailed and time had arrived to take them out and love on the two creatures. Cuz opened the cage. My job—to reach in and pull one out. I tried. Mr. Coon tried harder. He bit down on my wrist, got a taste of me, and began gnawing. My screams attracted my unhappy uncle who finally pried the furry critter off my left wrist. Today even a cursory look at those scars pains me. In all honesty, my initial official version of the wounds involved an accident while putting the chain back onto the sprocket of my bicycle. Once again, the real story surfaced years later. That truth spoken in a family gathering did little to lessen the terror of my hygienic, antiseptic, disease-fearful sweet mother.

By the way, Aaron, some of these letters require more intense thinking to catch the value than others. This epistle is clear—give loving care and don't do dumb stuff.

Passing on values with hope,

Paw Paw

An Admitted Mistake, No Big Deal!

Rehoboth Hill
Cane Ridge, TN

Dear Aaron,

"It's the computer era!" or "We live in the information age!"

Already, in your short life, you have repeatedly heard those expressions. You live in a unique era when many folks simply blame their goof-ups, or as you say, "That's not good," on a mysterious enigmatic machine named the computer. Truly a fantastic invention, the thing catches the burden of much irresponsibility. As folks hastily empowered the data demigod, many simultaneously relaxed a personal responsibility to be accountable, thereby eradicating blame. So now days, you fix the trouble by fixing the machine, and gradually much moral and ethical concern surrenders center stage and even, on occasion, has been written out of the life script of numerous folk.

Way back yonder in the post-Great Depression era of the 1940s and 1950s, most people used another descriptive term.

Generation after generation of parents passed on this old saying to their children. Mothers and Daddies with no reluctance called up the phrase intentionally with the hope the direct words would kick into meaning in their teenagers or even adult children, and he or she could specifically volunteer these meaningful words solely out of integrity. The expression? As usual with Paw Paw, only a story can make his point.

My father, "Big Milton," spent a period from 1917-1918 touring France at the government's expense (World War I). Returning home in January of 1919, Dad, weary of war, immediately opened his blacksmith shop, welcoming old customers.

During his first week back home, a drummer (salesman) wearing a coat of Mississippi winter mud walked into the shop. The man, consumed in exhaustion and anger, blurted out, "My car's broke down out on the Eddie Coche Swamp road, and folks in this town tell me you are the only person who can fix it." Dad's sign advertised "Porch's Blacksmith and Repair Shop." Relating this story to me, he just happened to mention that at that time he had never driven a car or worked on one. Evidently, a mechanical challenge intrigued Dad and he agreed to "see what he could do." The drummer left town on the evening train, planning to return the following week. The next morning, mechanic Milton saddled his horse, gathered a few tools and rode down into the swamp in a cold rain. Finding the Model T Ford, he built a fire and began examining the car. Dad had some experience with gasoline motors on a sawmill run, or gin stand. To his amazement, the old car cranked but "Henry's Universal Car" would not budge forward or reverse.

Covering the mud under the car with pine tops, Big Milton crawled under the piece of modern engineering and began taking apart and examining the transmission, drive-shaft, universal joint, and finally, the rear axles. Now by his labor intensive task, he discovered both axles had cracked and fouled in their sprockets. He carefully removed the damaged parts, rode back to town, and telegraphed an order for a right and left Ford T Model axle to Everett Hardware in Jackson, Mississippi. Two days later, his order arrived on the morning Illinois Central train. Later that frosty day, your great-granddaddy saddled up again and rode off to finish his work down in the swamp. He told his story with a laugh, "When I got it all put back together, I didn't have any pieces left over."

Crawling out from under the Henry Ford marvel machine and feeling good about the repair job, he cranked the rattling car and proceeded to take his first drive.

Aaron, at this point, I need to tell you about the great Model T Ford. The Ford Motor Company made more than 15 million T Models from 1909-1927. Mr. Ford used a new type of metal called vanadium steel, a product three times stronger than used by other American car producers. More important to this story is the challenge Daddy faced once in the driver's seat. He looked down on three pedals on the floor, saw two levers on the steering column, and wondered about the function of a lever by his left leg. After working up a sweat from using numerous combinations of pushing and pulling levers and pedals, he accepted a proven fact—this T Model, after all his labor, would only back up. About tuckered out and exasperated, yet unwilling to accept defeat, he tied his horse to the front bumper and backed the black T Model all the way into town and on to his shop.

He told me this story over 30 years after it happened, and I remember interrupting him with my question, "Why didn't the car go forward?" "Son," he replied with a big smile, "I had made a big mistake. I put the axles in backwards."

He offered no excuses. He never blamed cold weather. He refused to be the victim of his own experience. He offered just a simple confession, "I made a mistake."

Aaron, by the time you understand this story, I hope you will know the power of truth when you need only to admit, "I made a mistake."

All humans make mistakes, especially Paw Paw. Our mistakes can hurt people, cost money, and often damage relationships. Jesus, God's Son, never made a mistake. He forgives our mistakes. He releases us from our errors by His forgiveness and love. His way, through His forgiveness, begins with our willingness to say, "I made a mistake." This serious confession contains just four words that once spoken intentionally declare your responsibility for your mistake. Paw Paw saw his Dad as his hero. That day he told me the T Model story, I just heard the words. Years later, reviewing the story again in my own mind, I heard his *message*. I believe he wanted me to know that he was a mistake-maker willing to admit his fault, and he wanted me to catch on as early as possible.

Passing on values with hope,

Paw Paw

God's Good Dirt

Rehoboth Hill
Cane Ridge, TN

Dear Aaron,

Aaron hurt my feelings the other day. He told Mimi, 'Paw Paw is nuts.'"
Well, this letter may confirm I have at least one loose screw, but don't draw
your conclusion until you read *all* of the letter.

Dirt—that's my subject!

Common, everyday, God-made, dirty dirt, sticky dirt, gooey dirt, stinky
dirt—all the kinds of dirt that get on you when you're playing, working,
or sometime doin' nothin'. We, the people, big folk, little guys, all get
dirty. I am strongly emphasizing my concern because of a recent discovery.
Our family never owned a camera. Usually, Mamma anticipated the photo
opportunity and borrowed an old Kodak box camera from Aunt Bessie. I
found a book of mom's pictures of me made at many places at different times,
and on a variety of occasions—school, church, home, family reunions, Scout
meetings, 4-H Club trips, and in both basketball and baseball uniforms. All,
I said *all*, of the vast variety of pictures have one common feature—I was
always clean. I've looked closely, viewed the pictures at different angles, and
tried to remember the occasions for the photos.

My collection included quite a variety of poses. Still one common feature—
yours truly posed only for "I'm clean" pictures. I fear leaving such a pictorial
legacy may afflict your mind, even convincing you that Paw Paw never got
dirty. So to defy any misperception, I offer the following disclaimer: the
young Paw Paw-to-be in those pictures ain't the real me. I got dirty due to
work rather than dirty only by play.

Very early, before first grade, I entered the fascinating sooty, greasy, often
smoky world of Dad's blacksmith shop. By nature, Dad's work at the end

of the day left him greasy, grimy and sweaty. The work left its signs. Over time, I moved from merely watching his labor to helping him and found out that dirt doesn't hurt and grease washes off. While there was never any resemblance to child labor, Dad allowed me to experience his vocation, and herein began my appreciation for the mass of folks who bless my life today because of their non-reluctance to get dirty doing a job.

Growing up alongside my father, I wrestled with dirty United States mailbags we carried from the depot to the post office at 6:00 a.m. many mornings. When he took the temporary job as night watchman at the local poultry cleaning plant, I, by then a teenager, swept and washed the residual from chickens into an open sewer flow channel, sometimes up to 2:00 a.m. in the morning.

One summer during high school, a friend and I contracted to clean and refinish all the floors in our local school building. The process involved scraping up bubble gum and packed-on mud, wet-buffing the grime from the floors after the previous school year's traffic, vacuuming up the soapy, filthy water, and applying a shellac hard wax to finish the classroom and hall floors. The project extended through the June and July heat in a non or never air-conditioned building. One afternoon, I went back to check a previously finished room and discovered a bare spot. Attempting to cover the small area by reaching far beyond my normal arm length, I slipped and fell into a three gallon G.I. pan of shellac wax. Such baptism, while short of total immersion, covered most of my clothes, face, hair, arms, and hands. Having no available cleaner for such an emergency, I ran home in 90+ degree heat. Once home, I remembered that Mom and Dad had gone to Jackson to Mom's doctor. Fearful of my condition and nearing panic, I did a dumb thing. Because the wax was trapping body heat and I could not sweat, I got into a bathtub of cold water. Immediately, my body cooled and the sticky effect of the wax vanished; however, I was waxed-over and beyond the cleansing relief of bath soap. But God is good. In a few minutes, while I was bordering more on panic, my folks drove up, came in, and found me waxed into the bathtub. Quickly draining the water, Mom and Dad began dissolving the wax with mineral spirits while rubbing off body hair and patches of skin. I was a big mess. Later we laughed, and eventually I could appreciate my father's candid expression, "Son, it's all in a day's work."

Throughout this letter, I have avoided "dirt by play." As you live in a vastly different age than my growing up years, your best dirt hope may be play. So regardless of how honest work or play dirt happens, remember the value.

Jesus got dirty. I see Him alongside Joseph in the carpenter's shop, not merely observing but engaged in the task at hand. Our Lord referred to the validity of work with dirt and filth as he spoke of plowing fields, fishing, threshing grain, and herding sheep. Jesus passed on to us His gospel of work ethic and offered no judgment on honest labor by dirty work. Reflecting back to Genesis, I hear the Father's assignment to keep the garden, including a wide range of labor. Work, I believe, usually required the very act of getting dirty.

Now Aaron, just in case you haven't caught the purpose of this letter, bear with me a little longer.

There's only one way to express my concern. You and I depend every day on people who, willing to get dirty, help us and make life better. At the produce counter at Kroger or Publix, the vegetables and fruits appear clean, fresh, and even polished. Surprise! They all came from God's good dirt. Milk does not originate in a cooler. Somebody got up really early, lined up the stinky cows, washed their udders, and began the process through pasteurization, homogenization, adding vitamin D and acidophilus to the 2% milk. The grass and hay behind the milk came from God's dirt. I carry a burden that kids today live disconnected from the good earth. I am thankful I lived in the time when we dug potatoes and peanuts, pulled carrots and turnips, processed meat from the squeal to the skillet, and wrapped sides of bacon and ham with screen wire to keep the skippers out.

I could go on and on and probably will write again concerning my anxiousness for the multitude of children growing up disconnected from the good earth that even while soiling your hands blesses you.

Aaron, in our miles ahead and years to come, Paw Paw vows to help you stay connected to God's good dirt.

Passing on values with hope,

Paw Paw

Just Do Right

Rehoboth Hill
Cane Ridge, TN

Dear Aaron,

"Just do right!"

Passing through childhood and teen years inside the accompaniment of those words, I caught hold to their meaning, greatly due to observing scenes acted out in the drama of doing right by some of the main players in my life.

Living in a dry state, but more so a dry home, I never bore witness to parental or social liquor drinking. Our post World War II culture surrounded me with secondary cigarette smoke, but not in the house on the hill on Munsterman Road. Once Dad accepted a baby boy cigar from a friend. The Stogie lay on a shelf for weeks. One afternoon, he lit up out in the back yard and offered me a puff. I discovered upon inhaling the world spins both ways on your way to your knees as you throw up. So ended my short lesson on the evils of nicotine.

I cannot remember any lessons on sex education. I rather doubt the existence of the term around our town. Young caretakers of farm animals just caught on to God's creative reproductive process.

Rather, major emphasis repeatedly focused toward language, but not the king's best English. I'm talking about rigid respect for restrictions on cussing, cursing, and vulgarity. Each, a category to itself, bore both home and community disapproval.

Cussing, as in "He got a cussing," usually included four to five basic words and one absolutely derogatory four word term that quickly said came out in one seven letter word. A large brown bar of wet lye soap rubbed over a darling child's tongue guaranteed a minimum of three to four months' remembrance to avoid cuss words. By the way, a more just and accepted understanding also existed between discipline and child abuse.

As to cursing, even rough characters detested the label of taking the Lord's name in vain around a child. Vulgarity, the down and dirty stuff, and disrespect of ladies received no toleration, especially in my Dad's place of business.

My remembrances do not infer our community practiced clean speech 24 hours seven days a week. Instead, the kids grew up in a neighborhood of mostly respectful folks who never sought to qualify as a child's cussing teacher.

Today in 2010, our crazy world lifestyle revolves around the absence of ease and intentionality with which folks struggle to do right. Even sometimes no struggle exists. In such a time of apathy, doing wrong hurts more than just the doer. Ease of and intentionality to do right identifies the value of those better mind days. By ease I refer to the normal, everyday and prevailing expectation to do right.

In the late 1940's, stores began selling cold drinks--Coca-Cola, Dr. Pepper, Ne-Hi, Big Orange, and Grape in six-bottle cartons for a quarter if you had empty bottles. Many merchants would trust a no-bottle customer to "Bring back my bottles." Kids and grownups alike protected their image as in "He's good for the bottles." Once a bottle-forgetter, the stigma traveled with you all over town.

Our town needed only one bank. No one used or knew of personal checks. Bank customers paid for store-bought goods with counter checks usually made out and signed in pencil. The process provided ample opportunity for deceit or fraud. Very seldom did news travel around about check tampering.

Mr. K. operated a county general store a few miles out of town. A popular merchant, maintaining a well stocked store, he depended on Mrs. K. to keep his credit ledger. Many of the K's customers, tenant farmers, would buy on credit and come in to settle up once they sold their cotton or corn crops, demanding their labor throughout the spring, summer, and fall. Occasionally, a farmer would make purchases while Mrs. K. was absent from the store. Mr. K, limited in writing, would enter the items purchased by drawing pictures. One afternoon late in October, an African American tenant farmer came into the store to settle up. Mrs. K. read out the list of charged items, including sugar, coffee, cotton rope, flour, and a pair of Hames, plus a big circle drawn by Mr. K. Pausing to look at the drawing, she asked, "Albert, what does this circle mean on David R.'s page?" Mr. K. quickly glanced at the page and repeated, "A hoop of cheese." David R. spoke up, "Mr. K., I beg your pardon, but I have never bought a hoop of cheese." After a few minutes discussing the identity of the item, Albert laughed, "Oh, I remember, that was a grinder wheel. I forgot to put the hole in it." A hoop of cheese cost several times more than a stone grinder wheel. Mr. K. did the right thing.

But sometimes somebody really junked good and let me down.

Dottie H., a hail fellow well met, outgoing, steady seeming, unrattled, occasionally came by Pop's shop with a few plows to be sharpened or a broken hoe handle. As a gentleman farmer and man of other interests, he farmed a few acres of feed corn. Late one July Monday afternoon, he stopped by and jawed with a few customers before walking over to examine a newly finished, reconditioned Georgia Stock plow. New handles, fresh red paint on the plow beam, and a razor sharp new 12-inch sweep point with a $12 price tag sealed the deal, I thought. He paid Dad, lifted the plow across his shoulder and drove off with the new purchase in his pickup. Late the following afternoon near closing, he returned with the plow, complaining that "It's just too light for my mule." Weird! "Mr. Milton, I've got no use for the plow and want my money back." Silently, in absence of argument over any return policy, Dad handed him a ten dollar bill and two ones. The plow bore signs of washing and a few dried mud spots. Once Dad closed the shop that afternoon, we got in our old '41 Super Deluxe Chevrolet to go home, I thought. He drove out the alley leading away from the shop, hung a left, made a big circle out below town and drove by Dottie's farm. Right by the farm house stood two acres of waist high laid by corn with the middles run out and dirt high on the corn roots, all signs of the intended work plowed by a Georgia Stock with a wide sweep. Dad chuckled, "I thought so. Son, I would have loaned him the plow for a day to dirt that corn. He didn't have to lie to me." A few weeks later, Dottie came by again with plow points to be sharpened. Dad met him at the shop entrance, "Dottie, I won't be doing any work for you anymore; seems I can't meet your needs."

And occasionally doing right costs more than a lost customer. In 1951, Dad decided to move his downtown shop into a converted chicken house on our home place. Rummaging through a tool chest at the old shop, he found on the top shelf a smut covered Coat's Thread box. The container, about 3 x 8 x 1 ½ inches, gave off a clicking metallic sound when moved. Removing the lid, he suddenly remembered. Prior to 1930, American coinage included gold pieces in five, ten, and twenty dollar denominations. He made a habit of saving the ones he received as payment for work. The United States went off the gold standard in 1930, and the government called in all gold coins. Actually, law forbade keeping gold coins. He well knew he held a treasure in his hands. Nevertheless, he walked up to the bank, explained his discovery, and received only the face value of each coin. Today those coins would be worth thousands of dollars. He did right, apparently with little hesitation.

Well Aaron, tragically at your young age, already vulgarity and great confusion between right and wrong has risen up before your very ears and eyes. Sadly, I cannot offer promise of a cleaner speech environment or easier time for choices. I can commend King David's right words to you, "Let the words of my mouth and the meditations of my heart be acceptable in your sight, O Lord, my strength and redeemer" (Psalm 19:14).

Passing on values with hope,

Paw Paw

Surprise Blessings by Perception

Rehoboth Hill
Cane Ridge, TN

Dear Aaron,

Many good folks moving through hard times during my childhood in the post-depression era kept a watch out for surprise blessings from the Father.

One of my most descriptive memories of such a faith experience came by way of a peach peddler.

Back in my kid's day, quite often men and women would travel house to house selling tonics, books, cleaning supplies, brushes, and fruit—especially peaches.

Some sales folks met you with a lot of talk, anxious to bear witness to why your mere daily existence could not continue unless you purchased their amazing product. Medications especially could cure—well, you name it. Most medicines fit into one of two categories: 1) the rub on stuff, 2) the swallow-down stuff. While infrequently their products combined water, grease, spices, alcohol, and food coloring, I do not recall any one dying from the cure-all elixirs. One brand name salesman stood out above all others for integrity—the Watkins man. I bear witness, his tonics, especially Spring Purges, worked. Even more reliable, folk depended upon this salesman's array of flavorings and salve. A southern post-depression household cupboard, if at all financially possible, involved a Watkins shelf featuring vanilla, lemon, sassafras, and peppermint extracts. The Watkins salve worked on sore throats, burns, cuts, boils, carbuncles, the itch, wasp stings, scrapes, arthritis, rheumatism, gout, and bedsores. Watkins salve could usually be found also in the barn to treat horsefly bites, saddle rash, girth scrapes, back grubs, tail fly bites, various forms of udder ailments, and cracked hooves.

117

By the early 50's the peach peddler was one of the few remaining distributors making home deliveries. Usually, he was a fellow trying to make a few dollars by going over to Georgia in July, buying a pickup load of peaches by the bushel and hurrying back to quickly sell the perishable fruit.

Stopping by a house, he simply asked in a cautious manner, "Ya'll <u>need</u> any peaches?" Never, "Ya'll <u>want</u> any peaches?" Hard up for money folk appreciated his word "need." You see, everybody wanted peaches, but asking on the basis of need allowed a family unable to purchase the delicious fruit to defer without betraying their dignity due to inability to buy a $2.50 a bushel Georgia peaches. Courtesy, honor and respect, while today greatly lost, overshadowed most honorable peddlers. He knew everybody composed the "make it through hard times" time.

The peach man, a peddler, gave our family one of the best tasting blessings I hold in my catalog of memories. He drove an old green dented, dusty Chevrolet pickup and pulled up followed by a cloud of dust in front of our house one hot, muggy July afternoon. Seeing him come to a stop, Dad and I leisurely walked out to his truck. The possible forthcoming business transaction demanded the potential buyer not betray any urge to purchase to the seller. I heard the question, "Mister, you need some fine Georgia peaches? Only $3.00 a bushel."

Dad, rubbing his chin in a contemplative way, observed, "Gone up 50 cents a bushel since last year." No comment by the seller. Near the cab of the truck rested an enormous pile of fruit under the careful watch of buzzing fruit flies in circular motion. Dad walked over, picked up one, and the man volunteered, "Them's over ripe and I can't sell them." Dad responded leisurely, "I got some hogs." The conversation continued. "Well, brother, help yourself to all you want." Peering down at me as his mental wheels caught motion, Big Milton directed, "Son, go around to the back of the house and get both of those big galvanized wash tubs." We filled both tubs with over ripe peaches, and the two of us began carrying one—I thought—to the hog pen. Near to the back porch, Dad directed again, "Turn to the right, set the tub on the porch and call your Mamma." In a matter of minutes, we unloaded six washtubs of very ripe peaches onto the screened in porch and shooed out the flies. You see, my Dad saw the amazing opportunity for an abundance of peach preserves as yet unknown to the Porches. For two days, we skinned the delicate fruit. Being over-ripe, the peeling came off like skin with no knife peeling required. As Dad and

I skinned, Mamma cooked. I made three quick bicycle trips to Goodman's Grocery for Mason jar lids and sugar. In the 24-hour period, all available glass jars, both screw top and seal lid top, sat upside down covering the kitchen counter and table. As I remember, we ate peach preserves regularly for three years. The hogs *did* get the peelings.

Now, I suppose a question could be raised about integrity. Remember though, Dad only said, "I have hogs," and no commitment had been made to feed the peaches to the hogs. On the other hand, maybe there was a "gross misunderstanding." Nevertheless, the three of the Porches benefited greatly from merchandise that could not be sold, thereby lessening the weight on the old truck and also alleviating the peddler from improper disposition of the fruit, or even allowing the over-ripe peaches to transition into fermented compounds that if ingested could advance inebriation. Actually, I even as a boy sized up that peach peddler as a qualified "no dummy." According to my daughter, in her sweet mom's (my mother) version of this memory, Dad gave the peddler a $5 bill.

You may also debate whether or not this was a blessing from God. Any reluctance to understand such providence would grow certainly out of a lack of understanding of the times in which we lived. There was a strong connection between what God was about and what you were receiving on a daily basis in a post-Depression Christian home in Mississippi. Sometimes response to blessing requires quick thinking and just plain old fashioned savvy.

Passing on values with hope,

Paw Paw

Big MISS-OUT, the Wiser Choice

Rehoboth Hill
Cane Ridge, TN

Dear Aaron,

Jesus, the master pupil, challenges me daily to keep on learning. Aaron, I draw this conclusion from my understanding of Luke's summation of 18 years of Jesus' life. The Gentile writer noted, "Jesus increased" (Luke 2:52).

The verb "increase" really describes the idea of moving on and forward against obstacles or barriers. "Learning" actually refers to your personal push against the limitation of ignorance. The earthly Christ became well-schooled throughout His silent years.

According to Scripture, because of His great learning, Jesus spoke about a wide range of subjects including farming, fishing, politics, business, government, employer/employee relations, taxes, sailing, building, the weather, anger, love, gentleness, fraud, food, humility, compassion, history, respect, and especially kindness.

Paw Paw's quick Bible study hopefully can attract you to a big and essential lesson that once learned can increase the fun in your life. I call the lesson "Learning to Avoid Pity Parties." Now, I know you are meeting the early challenges of ABCs, 123s, and reading, plus computers, electronics, and video games. But please hear me out on the pity party lesson, and add my warning to your basic education.

Looking a long way back to my childhood and remembering my attempt to host pity parties, I now draw certain conclusions. A pity party enters your schedule unannounced when you realize you have to live without what you need, or even want, and don't like the restriction. Very few people will come to your pity party. Those who might attend to support you in your "oh neglected me" attitude will only add to your distress, and your own misery can damage your better feelings about the good person God made you to become. Finally, by experience I've learned a pity party can sneak up on you before you even send out the invitations.

Possibly by now you wonder, "Paw Paw, is this pity party stuff really a big deal?" Okay, I owe you my reason for this letter.

You are quickly growing up and entering into a world with an amazing availability of stuff and the allurement or seduction of the credit trap. (You'll understand that term in a few years.) I fear that your young years may bypass at least an invitation to the struggle to enjoy life with "MISS-OUTS."

My early life pity parties were directly related to what I missed, which left me feeling deprived and short-changed as a child.

Let me see if I can explain the situation.

I missed out by not playing high school football. In 1958, for the first time ever, my high school sports program included football. As a 17 year-old, 180-pound, six-foot senior—I was ready. The long wait was over. My announcement of intention to play caused consternation, tears, and a bowed up back to my dear mother. She was totally against it. Daddy couldn't care less. After all, football to him resembled a big fight. Mamma weakened a bit, even to inviting the coach to supper to "talk over this football issue." Shortly after the blessing spoken over fried chicken, mashed potatoes, corn bread, fried okra, and sweet tea, Mamma pronounced her priority question, "Coach, will you guarantee me he will not get hurt, especially his face?" In the midst of my lost appetite and full of embarrassment, the coach offered tactfully, "No guarantee." Years later he would tell me he knew the power of her question created a vacancy on the team.

For days, my innate leaning toward obedience to my Mamma struggled with my discomfort over losing the last opportunity to realize a long-sought hope. Far into my seething unrest and growing distance from Mamma, my quiet, wise Dad took me aside for a "talkin.'" "Son, this football choice is still in your hands. However, I have another choice for you to consider. You plan on going to college next year, and you know we can't help you as much as we would like to. What if you and I spent this year raising hogs, and you earned some college money?" In talking over the offer, he outlined the labor-intensive process. He'd loan me money to buy pigs to begin (repayable upon the sale of the hogs) and help me build pens and make preparations. Somehow, no really by the grace of God, I opted to miss out on football and spend the last year at home working every day after school with Dad. I never dreamed that would become our last year together. He died of heart disease the following year. I really did not miss out. Sometimes what you miss out on may open doors to big blessings.

I missed out not owning a saddle horse. Many of my friends spent Sunday afternoons riding their horses. Actually, their riding plans were included in our Sunday school class agenda. To feel included in the group, I wanted my own horse. The hurt lingered and deepened each Sunday afternoon as they waved while passing our house. Our family economy just could not include a horse, even though the home place included a pasture area. Then quite by surprise one day, Sidney, a very good friend, asked me if Dad would rent the pasture to him. His current pasture owner had hiked up his rental fee. Dad, knowing my yearning for a horse, suggested I trade free pasture for riding privileges. Sidney liked the idea, and soon Strudder, a Tennessee walker, became my responsibility in exchange for riding at my pleasure, any day except Sunday afternoon. Soon, much of the MISS-OUT feeling began to be drained away, even when my friends came by on Sunday. Thinking back, I realize I caught a lesson. My status connected to having something really didn't matter.

Now, Aaron, this last MISS-OUT will be written painfully as the story reveals a very little- known and embarrassing wound to my macho image. I missed out not learning to play the guitar.

During the opening week of school year 1952-53, a couple, man and wife, came to our town intending to raise our cultural level. They received permission from the school board to offer, for a fee, lessons in guitar and ballet. During a parents' meeting, the uppity duo registered children for classes. Actually, the meeting violated the Sunshine Law as no husbands/fathers attended the conclave. The town mammas signed up daughters and sons for ballet. The rural matriarchs exemplified great integrity and down-to-earthism and gave their kids a chance to play the Tennessee flattop box. As you by now have already figured out, the Porches lived in the city limits and I made the cut for the ballet lessons. This entire clandestine, unfair, reprehensible violation bordering on child abuse haunts me even today. Well, the other town boys and I hung in there for three fifty-cent lessons.

Then in unison we pulled off the Pelahatchie coup d'état. We revolted. We rebelled. We created mass disappointment for our mothers who then had to cancel the orders for our tutus (most of us needed a four four).

Aaron, sure, MISS-OUTS can be painful. Sometimes the situation necessitates unusual response. But most of all, remember to get on through your MISS-OUT and turn it loose. I believe that's even a way of honoring God.

Passing on values with hope,

Paw Paw

Traveling News, Community Expectation

Rehoboth Hill
Cane Ridge, TN

Dear Aaron,

Communication, or being up on the latest news in my home town, revolved mostly around response to one or two community respected questions, "Did you hear about...?" or "Have you heard...?"

News, loosely identified, included the latest update on lingering illnesses, a sudden death, who's in jail or needed to be in jail, purchase of a new Chevrolet or wringer washing machine, the preacher's Sunday morning sermon, couples unmarried to each other talking on the street, cars seen parked at Gip's Tip Toe Inn (a honky-tonk), a mother and kids boarding the bus at Cliff's Service Station, long Baptist deacon's meeting or Methodist's steward's meeting, anybody talking to old man P. in the bank over five minutes, a spring rain pushing the creek out of the banks, or what malfunction prevented the traffic light at the corner of Highway 80 and Brook Street from beginning to blink at 8:00 p.m. on Sunday evening, thereby stalling traffic following evening services at both the Methodist and Baptist churches.

In the absence of a town newspaper, our town folk depended upon the county paper, *The Brandon News*, "The only newspaper in the world totally dedicated to all the news of Rankin County." The editor chose reporters across the county who recorded the "dots"—a descriptive term for a column of happenings roughly confined to local communities of Lodebar, Sand Hill, Holly Bush, Crossroads, Pearl, Pearson, Gulde, Andrews Chapel, Rehoboth, Barefoot Springs, Shiloh, Mt. Pisgah, and metropolitan Pelahatchie. The county paper arrived in mailboxes on Thursday alongside *The Baptist Record*, the Mississippi Baptist weekly publication. These companion publications stimulated much interest and enhanced the focus on conversation throughout the coming week.

The county paper content centered around persons and interesting events and wisely protected personal dignity with a disposition to value the record of county life.

A few sample phrases authenticate my observation of the county paper:

- Boys interested in measuring cotton next summer must register at the courthouse by May 1.

- A.D. has been laid up with the gout this past week.

- Justice of the peace Earl J. discovered an unattended moonshine still on the Baines property.

- The Barnes family enjoyed a leisurely Sunday afternoon sitting on their front porch entertaining friends from Holly Bush.

- Pastor Everett took dinner Sunday in the Alford home.

- Rehoboth Baptist Church will dedicate its new attic fan during homecoming.

- The funeral service for Mr. Beaks included a touching tribute by his daughter.

- The Mary Frances Chapter of the Order of the Eastern Star's monthly meeting convened Monday evening with worthy matron Lillian Porch presiding in the chair in the east.

- Neighbors in the Gulde community have been hauling water from Edie Coche Creek due to dry wells.

- The bookmobile route next week will include stops north of State Road 43.

- Following a long church conference Wednesday evening, New Hope Church dismissed Brother J. and declared the pulpit vacant.

- The body of Pat _____, killed in service to his country while stationed in Korea, will arrive on the evening train next

Saturday. The family welcomes neighbors and friends to join them at the depot.

• The adjusted school schedule to enable students to pick cotton will be published in next week's paper.

Hard-time folks took life seriously. They practiced common sense and graphically described an uppity fellow, smart-alec, or a person failing to use his God-given smarts. Well known and well understood phrases afflicted certain folks, "Don't believe his mules came up," "He's three bricks short of a load," "He's like a lost ball in high weeds," "He ain't the sharpest knife in the drawer," or "He's all shuck with a short nubbin."

In a more positive communicative sense, the admonition, "His dogs will hunt" affirmed a person's work ethic. "He'll do to go to the well with," a phrase from the American frontier, denoted a well trusted friend in my home town. "Even a blind hog finds an acorn sometime" alluded to good luck.

Aaron, no orientation to communication during my childhood could be complete apart from waving.

From mid-March and on up to Halloween, most folks around town sat, rocked, or swung out on their front porches facing the street or road. Once the evening news broadcast featuring Gabriel Heater or Fulton J. Kalerthorn concluded, family folk migrated to the front gallery. During the eight-month period, the evening featured the fresh breeze of spring, heavy humidity of summer, and gradual coming chill of fall. Just sitting, offering few comments, and allowing the day to pass in review, all noble purposes, merited only a single category of interruptions—waving. Folks passing by, known or unknown, walking or riding, meandering or trotting, all without exception received the common courtesy of a hand wave. Such practice continued on the genuine desire to honor a person's presence. Usually a simple shoulder, arm, elbow, wrist, and finger wave set off a return wave, and even if just for a moment a friend or mere acquaintance acknowledged the aliveness of each other and even respected the God-given creation of another person.

The wave, while a cultural trait, if refused or resisted could set off quick rumor or wildfire gossip.

The above paragraphs only partially depict a normal day long ago. Since that era, clear channel non-static radio, no snow color TV, worldwide cell phone, vanishing slow traffic, most houses with no front porch, or empty galleries hastened the American migration back into the seclusion and cloister of the walled in houses. We pass one another as close ships on dark nights. The pictorial quality of TV displaced the fun of mental descriptive colloquial phrases and accompanying quick understanding.

True today, more words pass in review and we access information by fingertips with marginal connection to thought processes. In the ongoing quest to know if monkeys, whales, sharks, dogs, and pigs think, we have allowed the deterioration of at least the value of a God-given cognitive ability.

Are we better in communication? I honestly do not know. I do know of a time when communication made more sense.

Passing on values with hope,

Paw Paw

Immediate Response: Folks Need Help!

Rehoboth Hill
Cane Ridge, TN

Dear Aaron,

Yes, big and bad troubles sometime happen to very good people. You ask, "Why?" I also wonder why. Actually, I do not have many better answers now than I did when I was your age.

As I recall tragedies in our town, I remember more about how people helped hurting people and very little about understanding the reason for the devastation and pain. Evidently, the "why" became pushed aside for what our folk wanted to do to help one another.

Late one frosty fall night, the town fire siren screamed out, awakening most of the community. Many of us had no telephones. My father hurried outside and quickly came back into the house reporting, "I smell smoke, and there's a red glow in the sky down toward the creek." Fearfully, we got in our car and headed for the creek road. Two of my aunts and their families lived on that road. But nearing the creek bridge, we saw the G house fully in flames, beyond saving, and town folk huddled around members of the G family. Rushing out the car door, Dad cried out, "Did everybody get out?" The whole family had escaped in their night clothes. Even before the old house roof crashed down, neighbors were helping Mrs. G by offering spare rooms to the family. Ladies brought blankets to shield the family from the night cold as they reluctantly left the pile of growing rubble which an hour before had been their home. Mr. G and men of the town knocked down burning timbers and stayed through the night to prevent the fire from catching up and spreading to the barn and out-buildings to injure or kill their animals. By the next morning, the house place had been reduced to a black scorched spot in a frost covered field. The heavy air carried a peculiar smell. I recalled that same smell every time a house burned. No other smell resembles the odor. I suppose so many different household items burn together the flames give off a unique stench.

A recently vacated rental house up the road from the G place became their new home. A community offering paid several months rent. People contributed furniture, clothes, canned goods, groceries, fire wood, bed linens, and even toys for the children. I recall no junk. In our town, a gift to folk in need carried dignity. Even as a child, I sensed my fellow town folk responded for the simple reason—helping the G family was the right thing to do. Oh, I forgot to tell you, this was in the early 1950s and the G family was African American.

My first loss of a friend through a tragic accident happened on a Friday night.

We called him Junior. He lived with his grandparents and nobody seemed to know anything about his parents. He liked everybody. In those days, a 16 year-old boy could drive a county school bus in Mississippi. Junior ran a long route out near Holly Bush and Rehoboth. Rain or shine, his bus always arrived on time for school. He would even pick up folks at night for basketball games. On Saturdays, he cut meat and checked groceries at Goodman's Grocery Store. I never heard anyone say anything bad or critical about Junior, the happy, courteous, friendly high school boy. Junior's work enabled him to buy a used car—a 1950 Ford. As a natural mechanic, he delighted in tinkering with the motor and took great pride in washing and waxing his prized possession.

Down below town near Shiloh Church, a straight county blacktop road stretched just over a mile in length between the Lodebar community and the creek bridge. Late weekend nights the road attracted local fast cars. Junior installed dual carburetors on his Ford. Premium gas in those days sold for 31 cents a gallon. Late one Friday night, driving along on the creek mile, evidently Junior decided to push the Ford to maximum speed. Apparently he lost control, ran down a steep bank, and flipped his car. The impact knocked the motor loose and drove the engine through the firewall. Only after the sun came up on Saturday morning did a passerby see the wreck. Around 9:00 a.m. that morning, Dad and I went to town and noticed a crowd of folks around Goodman's Grocery. We walked over and immediately heard the simple, chilling news, "Junior wrecked his car and died last night." A whole town can mourn. An entire community will grieve. Sure, the whys came out. Rumors spread. I still remember the demolished, muddy car lying upside down in the ditch, and all of that really just didn't fit. Nice guy, hard worker, gentleman, now gone. And after 50 years, I still have no answer to replace his daring spirit.

And sometimes small towns and good people spend a long time trying to solve a mystery.

Early April meant warm days, but occasionally winter would surge through to stay alive, and the nights and days could turn quite cool. A family from Jackson came over to the lake near our town late one warm April morning for a picnic. The husband, wife, and two children had invited the kids' grandparents along for the day. Shortly after lunch, the grandfather decided to take a walk. After an hour and his failure to return, the couple went looking for him. After two hours without finding him, they became alarmed and the mother/daughter drove into town seeking help. At this time our town had an emergency signal siren. Two long screams meant community non-fire emergency. Volunteer firemen rushed to the City Hall and the mayor began organizing search teams. The group searched until dark. That night our churches held prayer meetings. The next morning, yours truly and all of Troop 66 Boy Scouts of America joined the search, having been excused from school. The state penitentiary blood hounds sniffed out the swamp, a National Guard unit searched, and prisoners off the county farm joined the search. After nearly two weeks, even with divers searching the lake, no trace of the gentleman had been discovered. Yet his son-in-law never gave up. Day by day, at least one and sometimes several town folk would go with the young man back into the lake area. Finally late one afternoon after over a month's search, the persistent, faithful son-in-law and my uncle found the elderly man's body face down in a little creek branch. More than likely, he became disoriented, kept walking, stumbled and fell into the water. Weakened from his walk, he could not pull himself out of the water. During the past month, the weather included near-frost nights and heavy rains. Possibly, he died from exposure. Actually, what happened to him is theory. But what occurred to help the family was the reality of a community that never stopped caring.

Such elements as these and others remain part of my repertoire of memory. Each brings back sadness. Still each reminds me of a place that showed me a bit of the Christ-like spirit in taking care of folk.

Passing on values with hope,

Paw Paw

Death, Dying, and Care

Rehoboth Hill
Cane Ridge, TN

Dear Aaron,

"He passed!"

"She passed!"

Two, two-word sets simply paired together announced only one identified message to the good folk of my home town—a death.

Aaron, your 21st century days offer quite a contrast with your constant over-exposure to pain, suffering, and dying while you abide somewhat shielded from the reality that real death happens.

Television plus various other communications heap more loads of death on you in a few days than I heard of in a decade. Except, in my home community, I knew death personally and up close in sight, sound, and even smell by simply listening to unprotected conversations about the death and dying process.

The death news spread quickly, usually accelerated by word of mouth due to the inaccessibility to few telephones. Along the way, the cause of a death whether by accident, following illness, or unknown reasons, ratcheted folks' interest up to intrigue. Suddenly, life in the community changed. Citizens of all ages, Baptist, Methodists, and the one Roman Catholic family, church goers, non-attenders, black and white experienced a genuine touch of the inevitable, inescapable to all lest the Lord reappear first. Within an hour, if not minutes, a rush to the home or place of dying seemed to seal tight our sense of community as the energy of the people blended into a help mode. One of ours, now lost, left a hole in the small community. So, a certain process, a local culture trait unfurled undirected by any one person but shared by the rush to care involvement of the town folk.

Among the first calls, possibly from the pay phone at the city hall, the only one in town, a family member summoned either Ott and Lee, Baldwin, or Wright and Ferguson Funeral Home. Each of these mortuaries, all in distant towns, catered to a different economic clientele in the respected order of po' folks, frugal folks, or the very few hoity toitys. By now both the Methodists and Baptist pastors had arrived at the home regardless of the deceased's denominational preference.

Once the undertakers arrived and expressed standard sorrow, they selected a time for the family arrangement visit to the funeral home and accepted chosen burial clothes (specifying clean underwear and socks). Quickly, a gurney bearing the deceased would be borne away by two men and lifted into the hearse. Two or three days later, six or eight pallbearers would be required to tote the casket. I never understood the change in man power. Funeral home arrangements, then a package deal, included embalming, grave tent, carpet grass over red mud if it rained, and the casket. The regimen of caskets ranged from cloth over wood, several gauges of metal, furniture grade wood (usually oak or cherry), and the optional concrete or steel vault.

At the selected time, the once body returned to the home embalmed as a corpse in the casket.

Pardon my interruption of the process, but a word must be spoken concerning the better dying times. Mid-March to mid-October offered a better chance to miss rain or cold weather. A Friday before noon demise usually meant a Sunday afternoon big crowd funeral. My dad repeatedly reminded my momma not to bury him on a Sunday. His reason–too convenient. He wanted his mourners to put out some special effort. He died early on a Saturday. Momma and I honored him with a 11:00 a.m. Monday memorial service. Dying Monday through Thursday limited the crowd to older folk and housewives, and quite possibly narrowed the musical selections. I'm talking pre-eight track and pre-reel-to-reel tapes. Most soloists and instrumentalists couldn't take off from work. So often, especially in the rural churches, only hymn book music and congregation acapella singing preceded the obituary and sermon.

Now returning to the routine. Once the family left to make arrangements, a local militia of community women swept, mopped, dusted, changed beds, washed windows, cleaned out the refrigerator, and attended to all measures needed to disguise all evidence someone had died in the house. The just lived-in look took over except for the clean vacant spot left for the returning casket and corpse. Occasionally men folk had to inspect the underpinning of a house to insure the proper positioning of a casket over the floor joist, thereby insuring support for the heavy casket. On more than one occasion, my dad volunteered his house jacks to level out a swaging floor for a casket.

Usually, the funeral home hearse delivered the body within 24 hours. The two attendants positioned the casket placing a pink electric glow lamp both at the head and foot. I do recall coal oil pink glow lamps out in the country beyond any electric service. Immediately, 10-12 black folding chairs appeared, each bearing the initials of the funeral home stenciled on the back, chairs designed only for light-weight mourners. A summertime death and a no window screen house required a viewing veil over the head end of the casket lest someone be appointed to fan the casket shooing away mosquitoes, flies, and other critters. Departing the house, the funeral home boys left a supply of fill-in-your-family name thank you cards, a white wreath for the front door, and the promise to cut off the cards from the flowers the following day just before the service.

Immediately, the initial family viewing followed the casket set-up. Comments included the need for more makeup, glasses on or off, hands folded or by the sides. This step cannot be undervalued. Once the family viewed, they officially accepted the corpse as their dead relative.

Late one afternoon, the Hinton boys walked into dad's shop. Dad, knowing his long time friend and their father had died the day before, stopped work to express his sorrow. They responded, "Mr. Milton, could you come over to the house? The funeral home brought Paw's body back and Mamma ain't sure it's him." Hastily daddy washed up, and still wearing soot and grease spotted overalls, followed the brothers back home. Once past the apologies for his appearance, he viewed his friend. Agreeing with Mrs. Hinton's doubt, he responded, "Years ago Coon (Mr. Hinton) and I cut a load of fire wood and his ax slipped and hacked a deep gash behind his left knee, leaving a deep scar." Assisted by the undertakers, the Hinton boys turned their paw over in the casket and pulled down his pants. No scar!

The funeral home had accidentally switched the bodies. Another family in the north end of the county was currently experiencing similar doubts. The body exchange occurred prior to time to receive friends. No hard feelings, no lawsuit, problem corrected. Years later, it became a big laugh and a priority hometown story.

Once family receiving time began, a steady stream of folks moved through the house. Men folk, having expressed condolences, moved out to the porch or clustered in the front yard while the women kept the vigil inside. Quickly, the two groups offered distinctly different conversations.

The ladies posed perceptive interrogation, "How'd he look to you?" "He looked pale." "He seemed puffy." "I thought he was awfully bloated." "He looks as if he could speak." All seemed reluctant to express the reality, he looked dead. Soon, ladies took to reading cards on the floral sprays and stands, mentally noting size, type of flower, and especially cards with multiple family names. Such flower tributes often received scorn as cheap. Oh well, all that floral talk would receive ample gossip the following Friday—church hair set day at Margie's Beauty Parlor.

Men folk rehearsed stories centering on their friend's life, and by 8:00 p.m., conversation turned to "Who's gonna sit up tonight?" Each man voiced willingness in varying degrees, and soon the old boys arrived upon a schedule. Young men or boys including myself begged to sit up. Such honor meant an early rite of passage to manhood.

The following day or two days later, depending on the visitation schedule, the procession to the church began forming. Somebody always carried jumper cables, a flat fix kit, hand air pump, and an extra can of gas—all standard equipment to prevent any interruption once the procession left the house. Anyone low on gas got topped off by a Bubba type who refrained on drawing on his cigarette while pouring in the gasoline.

Nearing the church, folk in the procession peered ahead seeking to size up the crowd. Oh yeah, a funeral during an election year added a good 10-15% as all candidates mourned.

The Christian memorial service featured the best possible response to requested music, selected Scripture, features of the life of the deceased, assurance of heaven, and a simple presentation of the wondrous Plan of Salvation. Pastors gave dignity and honor to the service, spoke with compassion, and called the community to aiding and bearing the new loss in the family. In the 1940s and 1950s, the sense of celebration even for a devout Christian had not entered the standard funeral service.

Once the service ended and the procession moved through town, merchants not attending the service stopped business, closed doors to stores, and assisted in developing a shadow of sorrow to creep over the town. My father considered merely closing for the passing procession a hypocritical act. To him, you closed tight and went to the service or stayed open, stood outside your business, and saluted the passing line of cars.

Cemetery sites on bare hills or wide fields offered little or no relief from sun, rain, or wind. Specialty graveside services could include military rites, Masonic, Order of the Eastern Star rituals, or Woodmen of the World readings. I do remember one service attended by members of the Ku Klux Klan—all in clean sheets and standing beside the Great Pubba.

Following the final graveside prayer, folks slowly expressed a parting word of comfort to family members. Usually, close friends received the honored invitation, "Ya'll come on by the house for awhile." Those words echoed more than a summons. The person had been chosen to keep a vigil of presence with the family facing the empty place in their family. The time to be alone had not arrived. The family wanted you near. The family needed you.

The town grieved together! And, borrowing a line from country music singer Miranda Lambert, "everybody dies famous in a small town."

Passing on values with hope,

Paw Paw

Now Home on Rehoboth Hill

Cane Ridge, TN

Dear Aaron,

Older folk ought to pass on good values to young folk. Hopefully, my description of the various people connected to my childhood will alert you to watch and listen to the good folk of your early childhood.

These real people lived on through their mistakes, crises, pain, limits, and effects of sin by the grace of God with a sensitivity to needs of others of their community.

Within a decade following my graduation from high school (1959), the gentleness of the times in a community alive with a relaxed pace had fallen victim to haste. Travel quickly. Communicate immediately. Provide instant accessibility to goods and services.

But as for me and those years, I strongly believe I grew up in a good place among wise folk in the best of hard times. To all mentioned here and many, many others, thank you for blessing my life.

Passing on values with hope,

Paw Paw

LaVergne, TN USA
21 February 2011
217325LV00002B/2/P